Junto Tribe Workbook

by Jim Marion

1st Edition, Sep 2024

Based on the Book "Seek Adapt Endure" by Michael Sanders

For more information about content placed throughout the book, email—
James.marion22@gmail.com

Copyright 2024,

All rights reserved. No part of this book may be reproduced in any form or by any means without permission in writing by the publisher.

Table of Contents

Introduction: Seek. Adapt. Endure   7

Week 1: Finding Our Way to the Authentic (Ch. 1-2)   1

   Challenge: Every Day Is Training Day   *4*

Week 2: You Are a Disciple (Ch. 3)   11

   Challenge: Don't Just Survive…Thrive   *15*

Week 3: Purpose Statement Exercise   21

   Challenge: Write your Purpose Statement   *26*

Week 4: Share Your Purpose   35

   Challenge: Find Accountability   *36*

Week 5: You Are a Servant (Ch. 4)   41

   Challenge: Love Is 1Cor 13   *45*

Week 6: Shame vs. Love   53

   Challenge: Serve Daily   *55*

Week 7: Jesus Washed Feet   63

   Challenge: Modern Day Feet Washer   *66*

Week 8: You Are a Warrior (Ch. 5)   79

   Challenge: Warrior Self Assessment   *82*

Week 9: Prepare Your Soul For Battle   89

   Challenge: Throw Yourself   *93*

Week 10: Prepare Your Spirit For Battle   105

   Challenge: Pray From Victory   *109*

Week 11: You Are a Scholar (Ch. 6)   121

   Challenge: Electronic Fast   *124*

Week 12: Beautiful Outlaw ... 129
    Challenge: Football Only ... *132*

Week 13: Still Beautiful, Still an Outlaw ... 137
    Challenge: SOAP Method ... *139*

Week 14: You Are an Explorer (Ch. 7) ... 147
    Challenge: Get Outside/Get Tough ... *150*

Week 15: Dwell in the Shelter of the Most High ... 157
    Challenge: Marvel at God's Creation ... *160*

Week 16: Walk with the Lord ... 171
    Challenge: Be Still and Know ... *172*

Week 17: You Are a Craftsman (Ch. 8) ... 177
    Challenge: Spiritual Gifts Assessment ... *187*

Week 18: Spiritual Gifts Discussion ... 193
    Challenge: Dream Big ... *196*

Week 19: Say It Out Loud, Share Your Gifts ... 203
    Challenge: Build Week ... *204*

Week 20: You Are a Leader (Ch. 9) ... 209
    Challenge: Find Your Swim Lane ... *211*

Week 21: Leaders Create Safe Environments ... 217
    Challenge: Seek Honest Feedback ... *219*

Week 22: Leadership Panel ... 225
    Challenge: Called Not Qualified ... *228*

Week 23: Be a Man of Action (Ch. 10) ... 235
    Challenge: Choose Your Hard ... *239*

Week 24: This is a Call to Arms!!! ... 247

Introduction: Seek. Adapt. Endure

Today I will do the following: Go forth — I am a disciple. Be useful — I am a servant. Live with purpose — I am a warrior. Challenge intentionally — I am a scholar. Discover new lands — I am an explorer. Create joyfully — I am a craftsman. Be an inspiration — I am a leader.

Man was created on purpose and for a purpose. Therefore, all men are at some level searching for purpose and meaning, and yet so many are struggling to find them. If we look deep in our hearts, we all hunger for growth and mastery of ourselves, our strength, and our skill. Unfortunately, many times, our searching leads us to popular movies, media, and society as reliable sources for why and how we should live as men. Could it be that many of the models we look to are creating simple, selfish, empty, small men who don't really know who they are, and are at a terrible risk of missing the robustness of life?

The truth is we cannot know who we are until we understand whose we are. We cannot understand our purpose unless we understand our Creator's purpose. We cannot understand true authentic manhood unless we understand that we carry the image of the only truly authentic man to ever live, Jesus Christ.

Man is a special creation that has been blessed with an amazing ability to grow and adapt. This study will inspire men to get out of their comfort zones and challenge themselves spiritually, mentally, and physically. The seven archetypes discussed in this study will help men discover themselves at a deeper level in Jesus, find fulfillment in life, realize their full potential, and discover ways to go forth into the world in order to pay that forward to their families, communities, and workplaces.

Adapted from the back cover of "Seek. Adapt. Endure" by Mike Sanders

Week 1: Finding Our Way to the Authentic (Ch. 1-2)

"The More you sweat in training, the less you bleed in combat."
—Richard Marcinko
Commander, SEAL Team 6

Introduction: Why are you here?

How do you face your giants? Why does the story of David and Goliath hit with men? Goliath was an intimidating figure who taunted the armies of Israel mercilessly until they quaked in their armor. Then along came a meager shepherd boy with a sling...

"Early in the morning David left the flock in the care of a shepherd, loaded up and set out, as Jesse had directed. He reached the camp as the army was going out to its battle positions, shouting the war cry. Israel and the Philistines were drawing up their lines facing each other. David left his things with the keeper of supplies, ran to the battle lines and asked his brothers how they were. As he was talking with them, Goliath, the Philistine champion from Gath, stepped out from his lines and shouted his usual defiance, and David heard it. Whenever the Israelites saw the man, they all fled from him in great fear. Now the Israelites had been saying, "Do you see how this man keeps coming out? He comes out to defy Israel. The king will give great wealth to the man who kills him. He will also give him his daughter in marriage and will exempt his family from taxes in Israel." David asked the men standing near him, "What will be done for the man who kills this Philistine and removes this disgrace from Israel? Who is this uncircumcised Philistine that he should defy the armies of the living God?"" 1 Samuel 17:20-26

As men we hope we would react the way David did. In 1 Samuel 17:11 the Bible describes Israel's soldiers as *"dismayed and terrified."* The world tells us we should be afraid. God tells us to be fearless because victory is guaranteed. The world tells us many things can be simultaneously true and we must accept all truths. The Lord tells us there is right and wrong, and we must be willing to fight for what is right.

Discussion Questions:

1. Our goal is to discover that unique battle every man is itching to have and harness our full potential in Jesus Christ to take the fight to the enemy. Is there a cause in this world worth fighting for? Describe:

2. Recount the story of the SEAL in the training room that wanted to heal from an injury to get back to work…to feel like a warrior again. Is there anything in your life that you're champing at the bit to heal?

3. Can you relate to the idea that men want to scale the heights, tame the wilderness, defeat our foes and leave a legacy in this world? What does that look like for you?

4. On page 13 & 14, The author claims that men look to the world to define their value. The world tells us to find our value in our occupation or in the opinions of others. When those strategies fail to give us purpose, we give up hope of finding our identity and purpose and embrace the goal of mere survival. Where are you currently looking to define your value? Your Purpose?

5. Read Genesis 1:28, *"God blessed them and said to them, "Be fruitful and increase in number; fill the earth and subdue it. Rule over the fish in the sea and the birds in the sky and over every living creature that moves on the ground.""* What do you think God is asking you to do specifically? (Hint. Cultural Mandate)

6. Read the first paragraph on page 19. If we are made in God's image, pre-wired with the innate need to be a Disciple, Servant, Warrior, Scholar, Craftsman, Explorer and Leader (All exceptionally manly and aggressive traits) why is our first step to following God begin with an act of surrender?

7. What are some adjectives the world uses to describe what a man is? How does living our life as Godly men conflict with the world?

8. Teddy Roosevelt said, *"I wish to preach, not the doctrine of ignoble ease, but the doctrine of the strenuous life, the life of toil and effort, of labor and strife; to preach that highest form of success which comes, not to the man who desires mere easy peace, but to the man who does not shrink from danger, from hardship, or from bitter toil, and who out of these wins the splendid ultimate triumph."* How does the idea of the strenuous life nest with God's purpose for our lives?

9. Read the last paragraph on page 27 about the connection of our Soul, Body, and Spirit (Tripartite Being). Is there evidence of this concept in your life? Describe:

Challenge: Every Day Is Training Day

Read Chapter 3 (Disciple) for discussion next week

Every day is a training day. We want life to be easy, but the reality is that stress is required to grow? Over the course of this study we are going to train each area of your Tripartite self to become the man God made you to be. We will seek, adapt, endure. **Seek** to understand our mission and invite the Holy Spirit to help us identify where we need to grow. Get out of our comfort zones and engage the challenges God asks us to face. We will use the tools and maneuvers God provides to **adapt** to a greater level of skill and resistance. Lastly, we will be disciplined to **endure** through hardships and commit lessons learned to our habit patterns so that we may face the next challenge. Answer the following. Meditate over your answers this week.

1. What are your performance strengths and training needs (areas of improvement) in Soul, Body and Spirit?

Mental Performance Strengths (Soul):

Mental Training Needs (Soul):

Physical Performance Strengths (Body):

Physical Training Needs (Body):

Spiritual Performance Strengths (Spirit):

Spiritual Training Needs (Spirit):

2. After spending some time in prayer, answer the following question again. Is there a cause in this world worth fighting for?

3. How does the Devil attack you to distract you from your purpose?

4. What do you hope to get out of this study/group?

"One day Jonathan son of Saul said to his young armor-bearer, "Come, let's go over to the Philistine outpost on the other side." But he did not tell his father. On each side of the pass that Jonathan intended to cross to reach the Philistine outpost was a cliff; one was called Bozez and the other Seneh. Jonathan said to his young armor-bearer, "Come, let's go over to the outpost of those uncircumcised men. Perhaps the Lord will act in our behalf. Nothing can hinder the Lord from saving, whether by many or by few." "Do all that you have in mind," his armor-bearer said. "Go ahead; I am with you heart and soul."" 1 Samuel 14:1, 4, 6-7 NIV. Every man needs someone willing to stand back to back with them and fight the devil. We need someone to emotionally, physically and spiritually cover our backs. You don't have to feel alone men…do all you have in mind, go ahead; I am with you heart and soul. I've got your back.

Prayers

Observations

Revelations

Week 2: You Are a Disciple (Ch. 3)

Find your purpose…Define your "Why".

"God's Desire for us is that we should live in Him. He sends among us the Way to Himself."
—Dallas Willard

Introduction:

1. How do you define your identity (ie. I am a husband, father, child of God, mentor, missionary, pilot, etc)?

2. What are your current goals and strategies for being successful in these roles?

3. Where do most men look for validation?

Play the Simon Sinek video, "The Golden Circle," on youtube:
https://youtu.be/OVnN4S52F3k

Sinek's principles are based on the fact that Humans are designed to be purpose driven. If we find ourselves struggling all the time, perhaps our problem is we don't know our purpose. In fact, most of us haven't thought about our purpose, or what the Bible says about it. Instead we focus on what or how we are supposed to follow Christ…and fail to understand "why." True life change begins right there at the center of the bullseye where our identity and purpose are.

In Ephesians 1:3-10, the Apostle Paul wrote, *"Praise be to the God and Father of our Lord Jesus Christ, who has blessed us in the heavenly realms with every spiritual blessing in Christ. For he chose us in him before the creation of the world to be holy and blameless in his sight. In love he predestined us for adoption to sonship through Jesus Christ, in accordance with his pleasure and will— to the praise of his glorious grace, which he has freely given us in the One he loves. In him we have redemption through his blood, the forgiveness of sins, in accordance with the riches of God's grace that he lavished on us. With all wisdom and understanding, he made known to us the mystery of his will according to his good pleasure, which he purposed in Christ, to be put into effect when the times reach their fulfillment—to bring unity to all things in heaven and on earth under Christ."* According to this scripture, what is your identity? **Conclusion…you are a son of God.**

Matthew 28:16-20 says, *"Then the eleven disciples went to Galilee, to the mountain where Jesus had told them to go. When they saw him, they worshiped him; but some doubted. Then Jesus came to them and said, "All authority in heaven and on earth has been given to me. Therefore go and make disciples of all nations, baptizing them in the name of the Father and of the Son and of the Holy Spirit, and teaching them to obey everything I have commanded you. And surely I am with you always, to the very end of the age.""* According to this scripture, what is your purpose? **Conclusion…You are commanded by God to usher the kingdom of Heaven to Earth.**

In Colossians 3:1-4, the Apostle Paul wrote, *"Since you have been raised to new life with Christ, set your sights on the realities of heaven, where Christ sits in the place of honor at God's right hand. Think about the things of heaven, not the things of earth. For you died to this life, and your real life is hidden with Christ in God. And when Christ, who is your life, is revealed to the whole world, you will share in all his glory."* How do you posture yourself to live into Godly purpose? **Conclusion…Set your minds and hearts on things above. Align your heart and will with God's.**

In John 13:34-35, the Apostle John wrote, *""A new command I give you: Love one another. As I have loved you, so you must love one another. By this everyone will know that you are my disciples, if you love one another.""* He expands in John 14:12, *"Very truly I tell you, whoever believes in me will do the works I have been doing, and they will do even greater things than these, because I am going to the Father."* What are the practical things you can do to fulfill your purpose. **Conclusion…Love like Jesus loves and do the works of Jesus. Our what is love.**

Discussion Questions:

1. Read Ecclesiastes 1:14-17. *"I observed everything going on under the sun, and really, it is all meaningless—like chasing the wind. What is wrong cannot be made right. What is missing cannot be recovered. I said to myself, "Look, I am wiser than any of the kings who ruled in Jerusalem before me. I have greater wisdom and knowledge than any of them." So I set out to learn everything from wisdom to madness and folly. But I learned firsthand that pursuing all this is like chasing the wind."* What does it mean to be "Chasing after the wind"?

2. Read Ecclesiastes 12:13-14. *"Now all has been heard; here is the conclusion of the matter: Fear God and keep his commandments, for this is the duty of all mankind. For God will bring every deed into judgment, including every hidden thing, whether it is good or evil."* Instead of chasing after the wind, what should we focus on?

3. Read Isaiah 53:6. *"We all, like sheep, have gone astray, each of us has turned to our own way; and the Lord has laid on him the iniquity of us all."* What ways do you continuously turn to your own ways?

4. In the Old Testament, the Israelites continuously turned to their own ways despite witnessing the fruition of God's promises first hand. Page 41 describes the vicious cycle they followed:

- The people would obey other voices besides the Lord's and fall into idolatry.
- The Lord would raise prophetic voices to confront his people and call them to repentance, but by and large, his people failed to heed these warnings.
- Judgment would fall upon Israel in the form of oppression from surrounding enemies.
- God's people would cry out to him and repent, and he would bring deliverance.
- Full of gratitude and praise for God's mercy, forgiveness, and restoration, the people would reaffirm their covenant with the Lord and experience His blessing and favor as a result.
- Yet within a few generations, the people would slacken in their devotion to the Lord and be drawn again to worship other gods.

Have you seen this cycle take root in your own life? Why is it so easy to fall into this same cycle?

5. How do you define your identity and purpose now? What is your why?

Challenge: Don't Just Survive...Thrive

Write down the answer to the following prompts...

1. Describe a time in your life, an activity, an event, a relationship, absolutely anything, that made you feel truly alive.

2. Describe a moment in time when you felt totally connected with God. Be specific.

3. What are some practical steps you can take this week to feel connected with God?

Next week we are going to explore our God given purpose. Make an attempt to repent of anything in your life that might get in the way of hearing God's voice. Talk to your group leader if you don't know how to do that.

Prayers

Observations

Revelations

Week 3: Purpose Statement Exercise

Introduction: Quickly discuss the answers to last week's challenge.

Discussion Questions:.

1. In what ways are you "chasing after the wind?"

2. Has there ever been a time in your life that you felt like you were living in purpose? What changed?

3. Isaiah said, *"We all, like sheep, have gone astray, each of us has turned to our own way; and the Lord has laid on him the iniquity of us all"* Isaiah 53:6. What areas of your life are you approaching with your own solutions?

4. What aspects or habits in life are keeping you from being the man God created you to be?

It's time release the garbage in your life that's holding you back. Put a huge X over your answers to the previous 4 questions. Your shortcomings have been washed clean by the blood of Christ. Get into the right mindset that you are cherished by God and uniquely chosen to live your purpose. Now let's step into our purpose to usher the kingdom of heaven to earth.

Purpose Statement Exercise

Write down your answers to steps 1-4. Pray over your answers and allow God to speak into your answers. After you have spent some time aligning your heart with the Lord and receiving your marching orders from Him, write your purpose statement. We will revisit your purpose statements at the end of each block of training.

Step 1: Promises, Prophecies, and Promptings

God is a speaking God, and He speaks in many ways—through the words of Scripture, through other believers who are listening to His Spirit, through the "still, small voice" in your own heart, and more. Ask Him to help you remember the various things He has shown you about your identity and purpose over your life, and to speak in a fresh way to you about them now. Write down the following:

1. What are the promises from Scripture that speak to who you are and your calling (list your life verses)?

2. What prophetic or encouraging words have you received from people who have called out your God-given purpose and potential?

3. What promptings or whispers have you received from God Himself to your heart reminding you who you are and why He created you?

4. What is the meaning of your name (Google it)? If you do not like the meaning, what do you want it to mean?

Step 2: Dreams
Our Father is the God of the impossible. Jesus told us that believers would do "greater things" than He did because He was going to the Father (see John 14:6). Our Father wants us to dream big about how we can see heaven come to earth through our lives. However, often our imagination gets shut down because of disappointment or because our mind has not been renewed to think like Jesus does. Make a list of your dreams. Challenge yourself to write down as many as you can. Highlight the ones that seem to really resonate with your purpose in life. If you find that dreaming is difficult, ask the Father to guide you and resurrect your ability to dream big.

1. When you were a kid, what did you want to be when you grew up?

2. If you could be anything in the world as an adult, what would it be?

3. What is one thing you want to do or accomplish before you die?

Step 3: Legacy
A lot of things Jesus did made no sense to His disciples, because He operated from a long-term vision. He didn't come to set up an earthly kingdom, but to leave an eternal legacy. He calls us to live with the same kind of vision, and when we do, it will directly shape our priorities and what we choose to spend our time doing.

1. What kind of legacy do you want to leave on the planet?

2. How do you want to be remembered?

3. What do you want to accomplish in your career (not just your current job, but over your career(s) in life)?

4. How do you want to impact your wife, children, grandchildren, great-grandchildren, and beyond?

5. How do you want to influence your friends, colleagues, church, community, nation, and the world?

Step 4: Inventory Your Values:

Core values are the fundamental beliefs that you hold in your life. These are guiding principles or ethics that dictate your decisions and actions in life. Think carefully on what you want your foundational truths to be and write them down. Memorize them and live them to the best of your ability every day.

1. What are your top core values (List 5-10)?

2. What are your primary gifts, talents, interests, resources, and passions?

3. What has happened in your life that transformed you into a better, stronger, more resilient person? How can you share this with the world? (If you've struggled so has someone else.)

4. Who are the people you care most about serving or partnering with in life?

Challenge: Write your Purpose Statement

To be completed outside of group

Step 5: Write your Life's Purpose Statement
Taking all the information you've collected through steps 1-4, write out a purpose statement. Start with a paragraph, then narrow it down to a sentence. Here are a few prompts you can use:

- My purpose is to bring heaven to earth by . . .
- I want to be part of transforming people's lives by . . .
- Successfully fulfilling my purpose in life looks like . . .
- As a son of the Father, my purpose is to walk in relationship and represent Him by . . .

After you finish your first draft, try to distill your purpose statement into one or two sentences. You may need to take a break during this process. Walk away from it, and take a look at it later with fresh perspective.

See your purpose statement as a perpetual work in progress, a living document you will update regularly through the years.

Use this purpose statement to set your goals. Set regular times in your weekly, monthly, and yearly schedule to review this statement. Consider posting it somewhere visible where you'll see it often—your mirror, dashboard, or desk.

Remember that you are more than just what you see in the mirror. God has given you a soul, body, and spirit. As you contemplate your purpose, keep your complete being in mind. It should be your daily goal to improve each of these aspects of yourself…Every Day is Training Day!!!

Purpose Statement 1st Draft

Purpose Statement 2nd Draft

Purpose Statement Final Draft

Prayers

Observations

Revelations

Week 4: Share Your Purpose

Discussion Questions:

1. Share your answers from the purpose statement exercise with the group. Are there common trends or similarities with the other men? What did God reveal this week?

Step 1: Promises, Promptings, and Prophecies
Step 2: Dreams
Step 3: Legacy
Step 4: Values and Resources
Draft Purpose Statement

2. Were there any surprises or connections from section to section?

3. What did you think about the purpose statement exercise? Was it beneficial to work through these thoughts in an organized manner?

4. Did you learn anything new about yourself from accomplishing this exercise?

5. Did the Holy Spirit reveal anything new about yourself?

6. How did the Holy Spirit communicate with you while writing your purpose statement?

Challenge: Find Accountability

Read chapter 4 (Servant) for discussion next week.

Read Matthew 28:16-20, *"Then the eleven disciples went to Galilee, to the mountain where Jesus had told them to go. When they saw him, they worshiped him; but some doubted. Then Jesus came to them and said, "All authority in heaven and on earth has been given to me. Therefore go and make disciples of all nations, baptizing them in the name of the Father and of the Son and of the Holy Spirit, and teaching them to obey everything I have commanded you. And surely I am with you always, to the very end of the age.""*

1. How will you use your purpose statements moving forward?

Share the details of your purpose statement with your accountability network (family, friends, etc). Pray together. Invite the Holy Spirit into the conversation.

Prayers

Observations

Revelations

Week 5: You Are a Servant (Ch. 4)

Discussion questions:

1. Recall the imagery of the sun as a servant to the galaxy. What is the world's definition of the relationship between power and service? How does God alter that definition?

2. What does the concept of "Mutual Self Giving" mean to you?

3. How did God intend for this concept to be used in the garden?

4. What is the difference between guilt and shame? How does God use guilt and shame to effect your relationship with Him?

5. Why do we go into "Self Protection Mode"? Read the list of behaviors on page 64. Which behaviors are present in your life?

6. Read Genesis 4:6-7. *"Then the Lord said to Cain, "Why are you angry? Why is your face downcast? If you do what is right, will you not be accepted? But if you do not do what is right, sin is crouching at your door; it desires to have you, but you must rule over it.""* What does it mean for sin to be crouching at your door?

7. How does God intend for us to "rule over" sin?

8. Do you feel compelled as a man to "never show weakness"? What are examples of this manifesting in your life? Have you built your life around the goal of never appearing weak?

9. When we submit to the world, we are telling the world we are weak and afraid, and that the world is more powerful than we are. Jesus never fell for the world's lies. How did he handle it?

- Luke 4:1-2, *"Jesus, full of the Holy Spirit, left the Jordan and was led by the Spirit into the wilderness, where for forty days he was tempted by the devil. He ate nothing during those days, and at the end of them he was hungry."* He faced temptation while in a weakened state so that he had to rely on God.
- Matthew 21:12-13, *"Jesus entered the temple courts and drove out all who were buying and selling there. He overturned the tables of the money changers and the benches of those selling doves. "It is written," he said to them, " 'My house will be called a house of prayer,' but you are making it 'a den of robbers.' ""* He didn't try to manage his public image. He was unapologetically a moral and just man.
- Matthew 12:22-37, *"Jesus entered the temple courts, and, while he was teaching, the chief priests and the elders of the people came to him. "By what authority are you doing these things?" they asked. "And who gave you this authority?" Jesus replied, "I will also ask you one question. If you answer me, I will tell you by what authority I am doing these things. John's baptism—where did it come from? Was it from heaven, or of human origin?" They discussed it among themselves and said, "If we say, 'From heaven,' he will ask, 'Then why didn't you believe him?' But if we say, 'Of human origin'—we are afraid of the people, for they all hold that John was a prophet." So they answered Jesus, "We don't know." Then he said, "Neither will I tell you by what authority I am doing these things."* He never felt he had to justify himself to speak truth. He did not fear what men thought of him.
- John 11:35, *"Jesus wept."* He freely showed emotion.
- Luke 23:39-43, *"One of the criminals who hung there hurled insults at him: "Aren't you the Messiah? Save yourself and us!" But the other criminal rebuked him. "Don't you fear God," he said, "since you are under the same sentence? We are punished justly, for we are getting what our deeds deserve. But this man has done nothing wrong." Then he said, "Jesus, remember me when you come into your kingdom." Jesus answered him, "Truly I tell you, today you will be with me in paradise.""* He generously gave to people in need without expecting anything, no matter who they were

How have you allowed shame to prevent you from following Jesus' example?

10. The world says you are the shameful thing you did (You are sin). Don't be weak. Overpower others…dominate. Success means others serve you. What shameful lies of the Devil do you believe about yourself?

11. Jesus tells us to face temptation from a position of victory. Who cares what the world thinks of you, please God, not man. Be vulnerable…show emotion. Give generously and expect nothing in return. Wash peoples feet (John 13:1-5). To become great, become a servant (Matthew 20:25-28). What practical steps can you take today to be more like Jesus?

Challenge: Love Is 1Cor 13

"When he had finished washing their feet, he put on his clothes and returned to his place. "Do you understand what I have done for you?" he asked them. "You call me 'Teacher' and 'Lord,' and rightly so, for that is what I am. Now that I, your Lord and Teacher, have washed your feet, you also should wash one another's feet. I have set you an example that you should do as I have done for you. Very truly I tell you, no servant is greater than his master, nor is a messenger greater than the one who sent him. Now that you know these things, you will be blessed if you do them." John 13:12-17

Before death, Jesus lowered himself for our sins. He wants us to do the same. This week embrace a lifestyle or spirit of service…the foundation of which can only be love.

In 1 Corinthians 13:1-8 & 13, Paul says, *"If I speak in the tongues of men or of angels, but do not have love, I am only a resounding gong or a clanging cymbal. If I have the gift of prophecy and can fathom all mysteries and all knowledge, and if I have a faith that can move mountains, but do not have love, I am nothing. If I give all I possess to the poor and give over my body to hardship that I may boast, but do not have love, I gain nothing. Love is patient, love is kind. It does not envy, it does not boast, it is not proud. It does not dishonor others, it is not self-seeking, it is not easily angered, it keeps no record of wrongs. Love does not delight in evil but rejoices with the truth. It always protects, always trusts, always hopes, always perseveres. Love never fails…And now these three remain: faith, hope and love. But the greatest of these is love."*

Explore what it looks like to serve those around you as a 1 Corinthians 13 man. Answer the following prompts. Analyze how you can be love in accordance with the scripture (be as specific as possible). Have fun with this and don't forget to invite God into your answers.

1. I display that love is patient when I…

2. I display that love is kind when I…

3. I display that love does not envy when I…

4. I display that love does not boast when I…

5. I display that love is not proud when I…

6. I display that love does not dishonor others when I…

7. I display that love is not self seeking when I…

8. I display that love is not easily angered when I…

9. I display that love keeps no records of wrongs when I…

10. I display that love does not delight in evil when I…

11. I display that love rejoices in truth when I…

12. I display that love always protects when I…

13. I display that love always trusts when I…

14. I display that love always hopes when I…

15. I display that love always perseveres when I…

16. I display that love never fails when I…

Read the answers to these questions every day this week. Pray that God gives you a spirit of service to "Be Love" to those around you.

Prayers

Observations

Revelations

Week 6: Shame vs. Love

Break out into small groups (2-3 people).

Step 1. Set the tone for the breakout. Read your draft purpose statements out loud to your group. Reminder…your purpose statement should include your identity as a child of God and your purpose to usher the kingdom of Heaven to earth. Remember your identity and purpose as you figure out how to fulfill God's desire for us to serve others.

Step 2. Recall the discussion on Guilt and Shame. When you exhibit guilt you understand you have sinned. When you exhibit shame you believe you ARE sin. Guilt causes us to repent and change our behavior. Shame leads to destructive behavior and feelings of despair. Victims of shame do not believe the truth…that we are all forgiven and redeemed sons of God. Victims of shame believe the lies of the enemy and keep us from reaching our full potential in Christ.

Step 3. What shameful lies of the Devil do you believe about yourself (See question 10 from last week)? What are your fears? What is keeping you from being the man God made you to be? Workshop it with your group. Turn these concepts into "I am…" statements about the lies you feel define you (ie. I am… alone, a failure, not worth the effort, an addict, etc). List 3 or 4.

I am…_____

I am…_____

I am…_____

I am…_____

Step 4. Share the answers to last week's 1 Corinthians 13 challenge. List noteworthy or impactful similarities and differences between your answers and the groups.

Step 5. Break free from the hold of the Devil.

1. What are the differences you noticed between your "Shame Statements" (lies) and your "Love Statements" (Truth)?

2. What are the connections between your answers?

3. Did you notice that your answers were similar to the other men in the group? How does it make you feel that you are not the only one struggling with these issues?

Play the "It's Not About The Nail" video.
https://youtu.be/-4EDhdAHrOg?si=a1B7YqaIDDd3pA4K
Remember…serve others the way they need you.

Challenge: Serve Daily

Your challenge this week is to assume responsibility for the emotional, spiritual, and physical needs of the people around you. Read your 1 Cor 13 Love statements every morning and commit in prayer to be the man described in the verse. Each day, perform one act of service for the people you are closest to. Write down who you served, what you did for them, observations about their reaction & how it made you feel, and what the Holy Spirit revealed.

Tips for acts of service:
They don't need to be grand, huge or complex. Remember from the "It's not about the nail video." You need to serve others the way they want to be served...not necessarily the way you like to be served. Communicate with your Tribe. Share ideas and remind each other to ignore the devils lies.

Act of service day 1:

Recipient:_____

Description:

Observations:

Revelations:

Act of service day 2:

Recipient:_____

Description:

Observations:

Revelations:

Act of service day 3:

Recipient:_____

Description:

Observations:

Revelations:

Act of service day 4:

Recipient:_____

Description:

Observations:

Revelations:

Act of service day 5:

Recipient:_____

Description:

Observations:

Revelations:

Act of service day 6:

Recipient:_____

Description:

Observations:

Revelations:

Act of service day 7:

Recipient:_____

Description:

Observations:

Revelations:

Prayers

Observations

Revelations

Week 7: Jesus Washed Feet

Discussion Questions:

1. How did the challenge go this week? What were highlights of the things you did (Share specifics)?

2. Was the challenge hard to complete this week? If so why?

3. What are some things you want to repeat regularly in your life?

4. Give yourself a grade. How would you improve your performance to get a better grade?

5. How would you describe your motivation for completing the challenge? Did your motivation come from righteous motives or from a feeling of obligation? Explain:

6. Were there any memorable reactions from those you served?

7. What downloads from the Holy Spirit do you want to share?

8. Read Matthew 20:25-28. *"Jesus called them together and said, "You know that the rulers of the Gentiles Lord it over them, and their high officials exercise authority over them. Not so with you. Instead, whoever wants to become great among you must be your servant, and whoever wants to be first must be your slave—just as the Son of Man did not come to be served, but to serve, and to give his life as a ransom for many.""* How can you apply this verse to the way you serve your family?

Feet Washing Demonstration

9. Read John 13:1-5. *"It was just before the Passover Festival. Jesus knew that the hour had come for him to leave this world and go to the Father. Having loved his own who were in the world, he loved them to the end. The evening meal was in progress, and the devil had already prompted Judas, the son of Simon Iscariot, to betray Jesus. Jesus knew that the Father had put all things under his power, and that he had come from God and was returning to God; so he got up from the meal, took off his outer clothing, and wrapped a towel around his waist. After that, he poured water into a basin and began to wash his disciples' feet, drying them with the towel that was wrapped around him."* What are some modern day examples of washing peoples feet?

10. Read John 13:12-17. "When he had finished washing their feet, he put on his clothes and returned to his place. "Do you understand what I have done for you?" he asked them. "You call me 'Teacher' and 'Lord,' and rightly so, for that is what I am. Now that I, your Lord and Teacher, have washed your feet, you also should wash one another's feet. I have set you an example that you should do as I have done for you. Very truly I tell you, no servant is greater than his master, nor is a messenger greater than the one who sent him. Now that you know these things, you will be blessed if you do them." How does this knowledge change your approach to last weeks challenge?

11. Who are the people in your life that you need to serve better?

Challenge: Modern Day Feet Washer

Read Chapter 5 (Warrior) for discussion next week.

Why is the act of washing peoples feet so significant?
- Builds intimacy.
- Builds Trust.
- Requires us to be vulnerable…both parties.
- Undesirable job no one wants to do…signals the recipient they are important.
- Displays commitment.
- Displays selflessness…no reciprocation needed.
- Perfect posture to discover other needs.
- Breaks down the receivers walls…opens communication.
- Perfect position to pray for the other person.

This week continue accomplishing one act of service every day for the people you are closest to. KEEP IT SIMPLE…GRAND GESTURES ARE NOT SUSTAINABLE. We need to learn to be good at, and appreciate, the small stuff. Continue meditation on your 1 Cor 13 statements.

In addition, every day, perform one act of service for someone outside the people you are closest to. Record in your journal what you did, how it made you feel, and what God had to say about it.

Act of service day 1:

Recipient 1:_____

Description:

Observations:

Revelations:

Recipient 2:_____

Description:

Observations:

Revelations:

Act of service day 2:

Recipient 1:_____

Description:

Observations:

Revelations:

Recipient 2:_____

Description:

Observations:

Revelations:

Act of service day 3:

Recipient 1:_____

Description:

Observations:

Revelations:

Recipient 2:_____

Description:

Observations:

Revelations:

Act of service day 4:

Recipient 1:_____

Description:

Observations:

Revelations:

Recipient 2:_____

Description:

Observations:

Revelations:

Act of service day 5:

Recipient 1:_____

Description:

Observations:

Revelations:

Recipient 2:_____

Description:

Observations:

Revelations:

Act of service day 6:

Recipient 1:_____

Description:

Observations:

Revelations:

Recipient 2:_____

Description:

Observations:

Revelations:

Act of service day 7:

Recipient 1:_____

Description:

Observations:

Revelations:

Recipient 2:_____

Description:

Observations:

Revelations:

Prayers

Observations

Revelations

Week 8: You Are a Warrior (Ch. 5)

Discussion Questions:

1. What jumped out at you about the chapter?

2. What is your definition of a Warrior?

3. Do you feel free to assert manly aggression in your environment or do you feel pressured to become meek, mild and tiny?

4. What are some things that suppress your ability or urge to be a warrior in your area of influence?

5. John Eldredge posits that as men we are, *"In search of our warrior's spirit,"* and that one of our core desires is to, *"find a battle to fight."* How do we find our battle?

6. Do you know your battle? Describe it.

7. What **tactics** does the devil use to prevent you from finding your warrior spirit?

8. How did Adam fail to live up to his calling as a warrior?

9. Read Professor Dave Grossman's quote on human aggression. Do you buy into his concept that there are three types of men (Sheep, Wolves and Sheepdogs)? Is it possible to exhibit tendencies of all three or are you locked in to one?

10. Recap the ways King Saul exhibited all three roles in his life.
- **Sheepdog**: Saul defended his people from the Ammonites.
- **Sheep**: Despite winning great victories, and being king, Saul withers at the site of Goliath. He enlists the aid of a teenage boy to defeat Goliath…a task that was his responsibility as king.
- **Wolf**: Because of fear, Saul turns on David. He plots many failed attempts to kill David and in the end kills himself in shame.

In what ways have you exhibited the behaviors of the sheepdog, wolf and sheep at different stages of your life?

11. In this stage of your life, are you a sheep, wolf, or sheepdog? Why do you think that?

12. Peter responded aggressively when Jesus predicted his death. *""Peter took him aside and began to rebuke him. "Never, Lord!" he said. "This shall never happen to you!""* Matthew 16:22. Peter thought he was acting like a warrior, but really he lost sight of what God had in mind. He thought he was defending Jesus. How does the world distort the definition of a warrior to blind you to God's plan?

13. What's holding you back? What actions or behaviors do you need to start doing with ferocity?

14. Do you agree with the concept that Love is the greatest weapon of the warrior? How can you start yielding this weapon today?

Challenge: Warrior Self Assessment

Take the Warrior Self Assessment and come to the group next week prepared to discuss your results. Answer the survey as honestly as you can…then ask God to show you how to be a sheepdog. Remember…you are a dangerous man. It's time to take on the devils attacks with ferocity!!!

JUNTO TRIBE MINISTRIES

I AM A WARRIOR – I LIVE WITH PURPOSE
Self Assessment of Needs

Name: _____

Please circle the number next to each statement to indicate the extent to which you agree or disagree with that statement.

		Disagree Strongly	Disagree a little	Neither agree nor disagree	Agree a little	Agree strongly
		1	2	3	4	5
1)	I am courageous in my upholding of gospel-oriented justice.	1	2	3	4	5
2)	I seek and hold up the vulnerable, giving them the dignity they deserve.	1	2	3	4	5
3)	I actively seek out the confused or lost to be a continual source of support for them.	1	2	3	4	5
4)	I am intentional about making sure I have Biblical alignment in my thoughts and actions.	1	2	3	4	5
5)	I am vigilant, serving as a watchman over the daily activities going on in the world around me.	1	2	3	4	5
6)	I am courageous in protecting those with whom I have been charged.	1	2	3	4	5
7)	I train and care for myself physically, mentally, and spiritually so that should the moment present itself, I am prepared to protect those whom I am called to protect.	1	2	3	4	5
8)	I have prepared myself spiritually to address moments of self-doubt.	1	2	3	4	5
9)	I have prepared myself spiritually to stand up for those unable or unwilling to defend themselves.	1	2	3	4	5
10)	I am brave and bold in my pursuit of Biblical Gospel-based truth and am willing to defend those truths.	1	2	3	4	5

Total score: _____

GUIDELINES for MASTERY LEVEL

Mastery	41 to 50	Near optimal mastery. Keep striving to be His presence in our world & encourage others.
Partial Mastery	31 to 40	There are steps you can take for optimization. Select a couple for mastery.
Progressing	11 to 30	Good progress. Identify a couple of steps on which to focus effort.
Emerging	1 to 10	Excellent place to start. Room for growth. Select a step for growth.

Higher total scores represent higher levels of inclination toward the archetypal category of Warrior. Lower scores may indicate an opportunity for growth. To evaluate your personal mastery level for the archetype, use the Guidelines for Mastery Level.

Prayers

Observations

Revelations

Week 9: Prepare Your Soul For Battle

The Dictionary defines resilience as, *"The capacity to withstand or to recover quickly from difficulties; toughness/grit. The ability of a substance or object to spring back into shape; elasticity."*

The American Psychological Association defines resilience as, *"The process of adapting well in the face of adversity, trauma, tragedy, threats or even significant sources of stress."*

Both these definitions define a quality that is important for men in their role as a warrior. As men of God, if we are to be resilient warriors, the truth of the gospel must also inform our definition. To be truly resilient, the truth of the gospel must inform our identity, purpose and our tripartite structures (Soul, Body, Spirit). We must develop a gospel inspired "disposition by habituation." In other words, when exposed to attacks of the devil, we must find a way to diminish our response. Control what we can...and let go of what we can't. True resilience is therefore tied to behavior. Our emotions are valid...as men, we are still allowed to "feel all the feels." Resilient men have the ability to pause their behavior when their emotions try to take over...the pause allows their positive or correct perspective thinking to lead their behavior.

The world, on the contrary, has constructed an aggressive argument against God and it focuses on a fabricated conflict between the Omnipotent, Omniscient, Omnipresent, and Omni-benevolent God.

Omnipotent: All powerful
Omniscient: All knowing
Omnipresent: Always present/everywhere at the same time
Omni-benevolent: Always good, Possessing unlimited goodness

What does the world tell us? If God is omniscient but unable to intervene then He is not all-powerful. If He is omnipresent but certain things happen beyond his scope then He is not all-knowing. If he's all-knowing and he's all-present, and he IS able to intervene but chooses not to do so then He is neither all-loving nor just. This narrative is a common struggle for men. But take heart...the truth of the gospel has the answer.

Discussion questions:

1. How does the world define the word "Goodness?"

2. How do you think God defines the word "Goodness?" What scripture can you find to support your answer?

3. How do YOU define the word "Goodness?"

4. Does your definition align with the world's definition or with God's?

5. Have you ever questioned God's goodness? Is it OK to question (wrestle with) God's goodness?

6. Read Genesis 32:24-28. *"So Jacob was left alone, and a man wrestled with him till daybreak. When the man saw that he could not overpower him, he touched the socket of Jacob's hip so that his hip was wrenched as he wrestled with the man. Then the man said, "Let me go, for it is daybreak." But Jacob replied, "I will not let you go unless you bless me." The man asked him, "What is your name?" "Jacob," he answered. Then the man said, "Your name will no longer be Jacob, but Israel, because you have struggled with God and with humans and have overcome.""* After reading this verse do you think God wants to wrestle with your doubts? Why would he allow that?

7. The truth is there are reasons far greater than you can possibly conceive for what God is "allowing" to occur in your life. How can you view the trials and calamities in your life in such a way that compliments the gospel?

Watch the Inky Johnson YouTube video:
https://youtube.com/watch?v=KjJXB2Zkxgo&feature=share

8. In the video, Inky describes the tale of two men…himself before the injury and himself after the injury. How did he define his purpose before the accident? What plans are you holding onto that prevent you from realizing your purpose?

9. Do you think God wanted Inky to blindly accept his fate? Is it OK to be angry with God in that moment?

10. How did he define his purpose after the accident? Would it change your attitude about your situation to know that God guarantees His plan is better and bigger than yours?

11. In Ephesians 4:22-24, Paul wrote, *"You were taught, with regard to your former way of life, to put off your old self, which is being corrupted by its deceitful desires; to be made new in the attitude of your minds; and to put on the new self, created to be like God in true righteousness and holiness."* How did Inky embrace this mindset? How can you embrace this mindset?

12. In Galatians 5:22-23, Paul warns that living by the flesh (Believing the world's narrative) leads to destruction. Rather we should follow the fruits of the spirit which are, *"...love, joy, peace, forbearance, kindness, goodness, faithfulness, gentleness and self-control."* How did Inky display the fruits of the spirit? How do the fruits of the spirit relate to resilience?

13. How did God reward Inky's resilience?

14. Inky said, "I knew I was doing what God needed me to do, when I was preparing to deliver God's message, and I got the same feeling I used to get in the tunnel before taking the field." What makes you feel this way…what gets you excited to "take the field?"

15. In Ephesians 3:16-19, Paul says, *"I pray that out of his glorious riches he may strengthen you with power through his Spirit in your inner being, so that Christ may dwell in your hearts through faith. And I pray that you, being rooted and established in love, may have power, together with all the Lord's holy people, to grasp how wide and long and high and deep is the love of Christ, and to know this love that surpasses knowledge—that you may be filled to the measure of all the fullness of God."* How does Christ dwelling in your heart, and being rooted in love, bring power to your life?

16. It's easy to stay mentally tough/committed when you are feeling emotionally connected to the Lord. Inky described commitment as, *"Staying true to the thing I said I was going to do, long after the mood I was in when I said it had left."* How does this quality affect resilience? How can you stay committed to your purpose when you're "not feeling it?"

Challenge: Throw Yourself

How can you apply gospel inspired resilience in your life?

Resilience and grit are a choice: *"Consider it pure joy, my brothers and sisters, whenever you face trials of many kinds, because you know that the testing of your faith produces perseverance. Let perseverance finish its work so that you may be mature and complete, not lacking anything."* James 1:2-4

The Lord rewards mental toughness: *"I the Lord search the heart and examine the mind, to reward each person according to their conduct, according to what their deeds deserve."* Jeremiah 17:10

Imitate Christ: *"Follow God's example, therefore, as dearly loved children and walk in the way of love, just as Christ loved us and gave himself up for us as a fragrant offering and sacrifice to God."* Ephesians 5:1-2

Work at it: *"Therefore, my dear friends, as you have always obeyed—not only in my presence, but now much more in my absence—continue to work out your salvation with fear and trembling,"* Philippians 2:12

Train your mind to focus on goodness: *"Finally, brothers and sisters, whatever is true, whatever is noble, whatever is right, whatever is pure, whatever is lovely, whatever is admirable—if anything is excellent or praiseworthy—think about such things. Whatever you have learned or received or heard from me, or seen in me—put it into practice. And the God of peace will be with you."* Philippians 4:8-9

Remember…"In life, some people don't need you to preach a sermon…they need you to live one."

This week intentionally throw yourself in the path of oncoming beauty. Train your mind to focus on goodness. Deconstruct Phillipians 4:8-9. At the end of every day write down the things you observed that were true, noble, right, pure, lovely, admirable, excellent and praiseworthy. Force yourself to notice goodness.

Day 1:
What did I observe today that was true?

What did I observe today that was noble?

What did I observe today that was right?

What did I observe today that was pure?

What did I observe today that was lovely?

What did I observe today that was admirable today?

What did I observe today that was excellent?

What did I observe today that was praiseworthy?

Day 2:
What did I observe today that was true?

What did I observe today that was noble?

What did I observe today that was right?

What did I observe today that was pure?

What did I observe today that was lovely?

What did I observe today that was admirable today?

What did I observe today that was excellent?

What did I observe today that was praiseworthy?

Day 3:
What did I observe today that was true?

What did I observe today that was noble?

What did I observe today that was right?

What did I observe today that was pure?

What did I observe today that was lovely?

What did I observe today that was admirable today?

What did I observe today that was excellent?

What did I observe today that was praiseworthy?

Day 4:
What did I observe today that was true?

What did I observe today that was noble?

What did I observe today that was right?

What did I observe today that was pure?

What did I observe today that was lovely?

What did I observe today that was admirable today?

What did I observe today that was excellent?

What did I observe today that was praiseworthy?

Day 5:
What did I observe today that was true?

What did I observe today that was noble?

What did I observe today that was right?

What did I observe today that was pure?

What did I observe today that was lovely?

What did I observe today that was admirable today?

What did I observe today that was excellent?

What did I observe today that was praiseworthy?

Day 6:
What did I observe today that was true?

What did I observe today that was noble?

What did I observe today that was right?

What did I observe today that was pure?

What did I observe today that was lovely?

What did I observe today that was admirable today?

What did I observe today that was excellent?

What did I observe today that was praiseworthy?

Day 7:
What did I observe today that was true?

What did I observe today that was noble?

What did I observe today that was right?

What did I observe today that was pure?

What did I observe today that was lovely?

What did I observe today that was admirable today?

What did I observe today that was excellent?

What did I observe today that was praiseworthy?

Prayers

Observations

Revelations

Week 10: Prepare Your Spirit For Battle

Discussion Questions:

1. Last week we spoke about mental resilience and grit. How did the challenge go? Did you find it easy or difficult to force yourself to focus on goodness?

2. How did training your mind to focus on goodness affect your opinion about how your day went?

3. Did you find it easier or harder to hear God's voice this week? What did He reveal to you?

Is Spiritual warfare real? What is it? We all have tangible examples of spiritual warfare occurring in our lives, but is it real and supported by scripture? What does the Bible say about spiritual warfare?

"Be alert and of sober mind. Your enemy the devil prowls around like a roaring lion looking for someone to devour." 1 Peter 5:8

"And no wonder, for Satan himself masquerades as an angel of light." 2 Corinthians 11:14

"You belong to your father, the devil, and you want to carry out your father's desires. He was a murderer from the beginning, not holding to the truth, for there is no truth in him. When he lies, he speaks his native language, for he is a liar and the father of lies." John 8:44

"For though we live in the world, we do not wage war as the world does. The weapons we fight with are not the weapons of the world. On the contrary, they have divine power

to demolish strongholds. We demolish arguments and every pretension that sets itself up against the knowledge of God, and we take captive every thought to make it obedient to Christ." 2 Corinthians 10:3-5

Spiritual resilience is the ability to sustain one's sense of self purpose through a set of beliefs, principles or values while encountering adversity, stress, and trauma by using internal; and external spiritual resources. What resources are defined in scripture and how do we use them?

External spiritual resources:
God the Father: *"Proclaim the power of God, whose majesty is over Israel, whose power is in the heavens. You, God, are awesome in your sanctuary; the God of Israel gives power and strength to his people. Praise be to God!"* Psalms 68:34-35.

Jesus the Son: *"My dear children, I write this to you so that you will not sin. But if anybody does sin, we have an advocate with the Father—Jesus Christ, the Righteous One."* 1 John 2:1.

The Holy Spirit: *"And he who searches our hearts knows the mind of the Spirit, because the Spirit intercedes for God's people in accordance with the will of God."* Romans 8:27.

God's Angels Army: *"When the servant of the man of God got up and went out early the next morning, an army with horses and chariots had surrounded the city. "Oh no, my Lord! What shall we do?" the servant asked. "Don't be afraid," the prophet answered. "Those who are with us are more than those who are with them.""* 2 Kings 6:15-16.

Your brothers in Christ: *""Again, truly I tell you that if two of you on earth agree about anything they ask for, it will be done for them by my Father in heaven. For where two or three gather in my name, there am I with them.""* Matthew 18:19-20.

"Though one may be overpowered, two can defend themselves. A cord of three strands is not quickly broken." Ecclesiastes 4:12.

4. How do you use your external spiritual resources to fight the Devil?

Internal spiritual resources:
The Full Armor of God: *"Therefore put on the full armor of God, so that when the day of evil comes, you may be able to stand your ground, and after you have done everything, to stand. Stand firm then, with the belt of truth buckled around your waist, with the breastplate of righteousness in place, and with your feet fitted with the readiness that comes from the gospel of peace. In addition to all this, take up the shield of faith, with which you can extinguish all the flaming arrows of the evil one. Take the helmet of salvation and the sword of the Spirit, which is the word of God."* Ephesians 6:13-17.

Prayer from a position of victory: *"for everyone born of God overcomes the world. This is the victory that has overcome the world, even our faith. Who is it that overcomes the world? Only the one who believes that Jesus is the Son of God."* 1 John 5:4-5.

5. How does each element of the Full armor of God aid in Spiritual Warfare?

Truth:

Righteousness:

Peace:

Faith:

Salvation:

The Word of God:

6. How do you pray from a position of victory?

Pair up in groups of two or three. Spend five minutes praying using each of the prayer types below. Read the prompt, share with your groups any thoughts or needs within each category, and pray aloud as a group.

Worship and Praise: Meditate on the incomprehensible power of our God. Contrast that with how close, personal and approachable He is. Think about the blessings of life and how He's given it to you. Think about all he has done through Jesus. Reminder: Not an opportunity to thank Him for the physical gifts in your life. Be in awe of the God of the universe.

Intercession: Plead and cry out to Him to answer the needs of someone in your life. Pray for those that are sick physically, mentally and spiritually. Pray for healing. Pray for God to send his angels and change the direction of someone's challenge in life. Reminder: Intercession does not cover your own needs. Think about prayer requests…all the times you said you would pray for someone but don't. Focus on someone else's needs and challenges. Share with your partner, say them out loud and pray for resolution.

Supplication: Pray for your needs. What is it you want God to give you in your life? Wisdom? Guidance? New Job? Pray God reveals His path for you. Reminder: First align your heart with God's, then pray for the desires of your heart. James 4:7 says, "Submit yourselves, then, to God. Resist the devil, and he will flee from you."

Thanksgiving: Thank Him for all your blessings. Focus on the good things that have been given to you. Show Him your gratitude. Reminder: Intentionally throw yourself in the path of oncoming beauty. Force your mind to focus on goodness.

Spiritual Warfare: Meditate on an area of your life where you feel the enemy closing in and trying to steal, kill or destroy. Recognize the attack and pray for the God of angel armies to send, invade, and take back the land that is teetering on chaos. Reminder: This is your chance to use all those big emotions and fire away at the devil…get mad, get mean and demolish the Devil, in the name of Jesus, as if he is a physical intruder in your home. You are a dangerous man for the Kingdom…act like it.

Challenge: Pray From Victory

Read Chapter 6 (Scholar) for discussion next week.

Commit to changing the way you pray. This week pray from a position of victory. Pray every day using the five techniques discussed in the prayer exercise. Record what you prayed each day, what God revealed, and any observations from the exercise. Be prepared to discuss your findings in group.

Some things to remember as you commit to this prayer challenge.
- Pray FROM a position of victory, not FOR victory. Use active voice (ie. Thank God for forgiveness instead of asking Him for forgiveness).
- Understand the big picture that you're in a war, not just a battle. This is God's war, but it's your battle.
- Don't underestimate the enemy, but don't overestimate him either
- Live under accountability...be around brothers and sisters in Christ.
- You're not man enough to defeat Satan on your own. Read Jude 1:9, *"But even the archangel Michael, when he was disputing with the devil about the body of Moses, did not himself dare to condemn him for slander but said, "The Lord rebuke you!""* Jesus is THE MAN!!!

Day 1:
Worship and Praise:

Intercession:

Supplication:

Thanksgiving:

Spiritual Warfare:

Revelations:

Observations:

Day 2:
Worship and Praise:

Intercession:

Supplication:

Thanksgiving:

Spiritual Warfare:

Revelations:

Observations:

Day 3:
Worship and Praise:

Intercession:

Supplication:

Thanksgiving:

Spiritual Warfare:

Revelations:

Observations:

Day 4:
Worship and Praise:

Intercession:

Supplication:

Thanksgiving:

Spiritual Warfare:

Revelations:

Observations:

Day 5:
Worship and Praise:

Intercession:

Supplication:

Thanksgiving:

Spiritual Warfare:

Revelations:

Observations:

Day 6:
Worship and Praise:

Intercession:

Supplication:

Thanksgiving:

Spiritual Warfare:

Revelations:

Observations:

Day 7:
Worship and Praise:

Intercession:

Supplication:

Thanksgiving:

Spiritual Warfare:

Revelations:

Observations:

Prayers

Observations

Revelations

Week 11: You Are a Scholar (Ch. 6)

Discussion Questions:

1. God created us in His own image and granted us dominion over creation. The Hebrew definition of dominion is: prevail against, to reign, to rule. What did God have in mind when He granted man dominion over the earth?

2. Read Romans 1:18-25, 28-32. *"The wrath of God is being revealed from heaven against all the godlessness and wickedness of people, who suppress the truth by their wickedness, since what may be known about God is plain to them, because God has made it plain to them. For since the creation of the world God's invisible qualities—his eternal power and divine nature—have been clearly seen, being understood from what has been made, so that people are without excuse. For although they knew God, they neither glorified him as God nor gave thanks to him, but their thinking became futile and their foolish hearts were darkened. Although they claimed to be wise, they became fools and exchanged the glory of the immortal God for images made to look like a mortal human being and birds and animals and reptiles. Therefore God gave them over in the sinful desires of their hearts to sexual impurity for the degrading of their bodies with one another. They exchanged the truth about God for a lie, and worshiped and served created things rather than the Creator—who is forever praised. Amen. Furthermore, just as they did not think it worthwhile to retain the knowledge of God, so God gave them over to a depraved mind, so that they do what ought not to be done. They have become filled with every kind of wickedness, evil, greed and depravity. They are full of envy, murder, strife, deceit and malice. They are gossips, slanderers, God-haters, insolent, arrogant and boastful; they invent ways of doing evil; they disobey their parents; they have no understanding, no fidelity, no love, no mercy. Although they know God's righteous decree that those who do such things deserve death, they not only continue to do these very things but also approve of those who practice them."*

Why would God give us dominion over the Garden but forbid us from eating from the "Tree of the knowledge of good and evil"?

3. How does the concept of "Free Will" factor into our pursuit of knowledge?

4. Read the following quote. *"Humans knew God…but neither glorified Him as God nor gave thanks to Him. Their knowledge did not lead them to the proper response: worship* (Seek, Adapt, Endure pg. 103). How can the pursuit of knowledge be used as a method of worship?

5. How can the pursuit of knowledge be twisted into something inappropriate or evil?

6. Read Romans 12:1-2. *"Therefore, I urge you, brothers and sisters, in view of God's mercy, to offer your bodies as a living sacrifice, holy and pleasing to God—this is your true and proper worship. Do not conform to the pattern of this world, but be transformed by the renewing of your mind. Then you will be able to test and approve what God's will is—his good, pleasing and perfect will."* Why does God want us to seek wisdom… especially Godly wisdom?

7. What is the difference between Wisdom and Knowledge? How does the difference between Wisdom and Knowledge get distorted to lead you away from God's desire for your life?

8. How does the world and our sin nature prevent us from seeking Godly wisdom? List some examples in your life.

9. What does it mean to "renew your mind," in Romans 12, in order to reveal your purpose?

10. Read your purpose statement. How can you incorporate the pursuit of wisdom into your purpose? What would you add to your purpose statement?

Challenge: Electronic Fast

Why do we need to seek wisdom as Godly men?
- Wisdom leads to influence
- Wisdom leads to obedience
- Wisdom leads to relationship
- Wisdom leads to revelation and PURPOSE!!!

This week fast from electronic entertainment and instead read the book "Beautiful Outlaw" by John Eldredge. Make this a Monday-Friday challenge. God would not want to deprive you of football...so neither do we. Read as much as you can in a week, but come prepared next week to discuss the first 4 chapters.

1. What stood out to you in the book?

2. What were the common themes that apply to your life?

3. What did you learn about Jesus that you didn't know before?

4. How did fasting from electronics affect your relationship with God, your family and your friends?

Prayers

Observations

Revelations

Week 12: Beautiful Outlaw

Discuss the first four chapters of "Beautiful Outlaw" by John Eldredge.

Discussion questions:

1. How's it going with your fast from electronic entertainment? Give yourself a grade. Explain:

2. Have you learned anything about yourself or others around you from this experience?

3. What are your general impressions of the first 4 chapters of "Beautiful Outlaw?" What jumped out to you from the reading?

4. Do you believe that Jesus is a tangible being that wants a personal connection with you? What role does religion play in that relationship?

5. Why did Jesus have to come to earth in the form of a man? What does that mean for your relationship with Him?

6. On page 23, Eldredge says, "*After all…it was God who gave us a sense of humor. Do you really think Jesus came to take it away?*" Do you think that Jesus liked a good joke? How does that change the way you interact with Him?

7. Eldredge describes the way Jesus revealed himself to the disciples after the resurrection as "Playful." Why might Jesus choose a playful act to reveal Himself in such a somber moment? How much did His relationship and history play into this methodology?

8. Jesus spent the better part of His childhood being hardened/prepared for His destiny (fleeing from physical harm). Why was that necessary for His ministry?

9. Jesus is sometimes referred to as meek and mild. Read John 2:14-15. *"In the temple courts he found people selling cattle, sheep and doves, and others sitting at tables exchanging money. So he made a whip out of cords, and drove all from the temple courts, both sheep and cattle; he scattered the coins of the money changers and overturned their tables."* Could Jesus have whipped (literally) the temple into a frenzy if he was meek and mild? How does that change your view of Jesus as a man?

10. How does Jesus' example of "Fierce Intention" change your outlook on your role as a Christian man?

11. Read John 11:43. *"When he had said this, Jesus called in a loud voice, "Lazarus, come out!""* Imagine Jesus commanding his friend to life in a thunderous voice. What kind of voice do you use in your prayer life?

12. Read Matthew 28:18-20. *"Then Jesus came to them and said, "All authority in heaven and on earth has been given to me. Therefore go and make disciples of all nations, baptizing them in the name of the Father and of the Son and of the Holy Spirit, and teaching them to obey everything I have commanded you. And surely I am with you always, to the very end of the age.""* Have you ever considered that you have been granted all authority in heaven and on earth? How does this knowledge change your approach to prayer?

Challenge: Football Only

Read Chapter 7 (Explorer) for discussion next week.

Continue to fast from electronic entertainment and instead read the book "Beautiful Outlaw" by John Eldredge. Make this a Monday-Friday challenge…you still get a football pass. Read as much as you can in a week, but come prepared next week to discuss the next 4 chapters.

1. What stood out to you in the book?

2. What were the common themes that apply to your life?

3. What did you learn about Jesus that you didn't know before?

4. How did fasting from electronics affect your relationship with God, your family and your friends?

Take a look at your purpose statement and make changes if you feel led to do so. If you make changes, share them with your tribe so the group can continue praying for your purpose.

Prayers

Observations

Revelations

Week 13: Still Beautiful, Still an Outlaw

Discussion Questions (Open Discussion):

1. What major takeaways did you note from the book "Beautiful Outlaw?"

2. Do you find it difficult to study scripture? Why?

3. Do you have a method for studying scripture effectively?

Scripture Exercise:

Below is a practical way to read and comprehend scripture. This is just one method that may help. Follow the SOAP acronym:

S — Scripture: Read the verse in context. Read the background contained in the intro of most study Bibles. You can also search for content on line. Note who wrote the book, who they were talking to, and the time period the verse was written. Read any cross referenced verses contained in the footnotes of your Bible. Look up any definitions of words you do not understand. Often times it helps to look up the Hebrew meanings of key words in the scripture.

O — Observations: What jumps out to you practically. Look for names of God which may point to certain attributes God wants you to apply to the verse. Underline or highlight any words that are repeated...this may imply emphasis or importance and change the way you perceive the verse (Hint...they are repeated for a reason).

A — Application: What did you learn from the verse. Focus on things you did not know before reading the verse. Write down some small practical ways you can apply the verse to your own life. Record what comes to mind. Make an attempt to write out the meaning/message of the verse. Write down your questions.

P — Prayer: Meditate on the verse. Ask God to fill in the gaps in your understanding. Ask Him to specifically reveal what He wants you to take from the scripture. Maybe make an attempt to memorize the verse.

Tips: Start with a blank sheet of paper and write everything down. Come back to it later if you get stuck.

Break out in groups of 2-3 people and practice. Pick a scripture and attempt the SOAP method to analyze as a group.

Scripture:

Observations:

Applications:

Prayer:

Challenge: SOAP Method

This week practice reading scripture using the SOAP method. At least three days this week pick a verse and practice this method. Be prepared to share something you learned with the group.

Day 1:
Scripture:

Observations:

Applications:

Prayers:

Day 2:
Scripture:

Observations:

Applications:

Prayers:

Day 3:
Scripture:

Observations:

Applications:

Prayers:

Prayers

Observations

Revelations

Week 14: You Are an Explorer (Ch. 7)

Find a beautiful place in nature to hold group. Get away from your normal meeting spot.

How does God speak to YOU?

God speaks to us through scripture: *"All Scripture is inspired by God and is useful to teach us what is true and to make us realize what is wrong in our lives. It corrects us when we are wrong and teaches us to do what is right. God uses it to prepare and equip his people to do every good work."* 2 Timothy 3:16-17

God speaks to us through music: *"After consulting the people, the king appointed singers to walk ahead of the army, singing to the Lord and praising him for his holy splendor. This is what they sang: "Give thanks to the Lord; his faithful love endures forever!""* 2 Chronicles 20:21

God speaks to us through teachers/other believers: *"In his grace, God has given us different gifts for doing certain things well. So if God has given you the ability to prophesy, speak out with as much faith as God has given you. If your gift is serving others, serve them well. If you are a teacher, teach well. If your gift is to encourage others, be encouraging. If it is giving, give generously. If God has given you leadership ability, take the responsibility seriously. And if you have a gift for showing kindness to others, do it gladly."* Romans 12:6-8

God speaks to us through our rebellion: *"Before I was afflicted I went astray, but now I obey your word. You are good, and what you do is good; teach me your decrees."* Psalms 119:67-68.

God speaks to us through difficulties: *"Dear brothers and sisters, when troubles of any kind come your way, consider it an opportunity for great joy. For you know that when your faith is tested, your endurance has a chance to grow. So let it grow, for when your endurance is fully developed, you will be perfect and complete, needing nothing."* James 1:2-4

God speaks to us through his son, Jesus Christ: *"So Jesus told them, "My message is not my own; it comes from God who sent me."* John 7:16

God speaks to us through the Holy Spirit: *"But when the Father sends the Advocate as my representative—that is, the Holy Spirit—he will teach you everything and will remind you of everything I have told you."* John 14:26

God speaks to us through nature and His creation: *"The heavens proclaim the glory of God. The skies display his craftsmanship. Day after day they continue to speak; night after night they make him known."* Psalm 19:1-2

God speaks to us through prayer: *"But when you pray, go away by yourself, shut the door behind you, and pray to your Father in private. Then your Father, who sees everything, will reward you. "When you pray, don't babble on and on as the Gentiles do. They think their prayers are answered merely by repeating their words again and again. Don't be like them, for your Father knows exactly what you need even before you ask him!"*
Matthew 6:6-8

Through other means…but never in disagreement with the Bible: *"For God speaks again and again, though people do not recognize it."* Job 33:14

Discussion Questions:

1. How does God speak to you? Be specific.

2. Why do you think God brought all the animals before Adam to name them?

3. Do you agree with the concept that the wilderness is a proving ground where Man finds his dependence on God? Do you have any examples in your life?

4. Have you ever viewed God's creation as a quiet place to be in His presence?

5. What distractions/shortcomings in your life prevent you from hearing God's voice (Ex. Wrong attitudes, unconfessed sin, resentment, choice)?

6. Can you recall any Old Testament heroes that fled to the wilderness? Why did they need to flee to the wild and what benefits did the wilderness provide?

7. How did Jesus handle his time alone in the wilderness (pg 126)? What lessons can you adopt from his example?

8. Read the Stephen Mansfield quote on page 128 regarding Roosevelt's concept of the strenuous life.

"All men need what Roosevelt found—a strenuous physical life, the possibility of harm, challenges to face, enemies to oppose, land to conquer. Our lives push us away from this. We work in cubicles or comfortable vehicles. Technology serves us and keeps us from exertion. We live in opulent blandness—overfed, over-tended, over-entertained, and overly preoccupied with ourselves. But men need contest and conquest, strain and struggle. Otherwise, we lose ourselves in softness and effeminacy."

— *Stephen Mansfield*

Is this true in your life? What steps can you take to satisfy your need as a man for a "strenuous life?"

Challenge: Get Outside/Get Tough

Spend at least 30 minutes a day outside and alone with zero distractions. It's gonna be difficult to cordon off the time…do it anyway. What do you notice about the world around you? What is right in front of you that you find beautiful or amazing? Pray. Listen to God's voice. Write down what he reveals. Answer the following questions:

Do you possess all the elements of the strenuous physical life defined by Stephen Mansfield? Explain?

1. The possibility of harm? Something that peaks your adrenaline/raises your heart rate?

2. Challenges to face? A goal that is difficult to achieve?

3. Enemies to oppose? A cause greater than yourself?

4. Land to conquer? New frontier to explore?

5. Has your life pushed you away from the strenuous life toward "opulent blandness"?

6. How does technology keep you from your purpose? Which technologies are the root cause?

7. How are you overfed? What small change in your life can you implement to change this?

8. Are you over-tended? How have you been softened by your circumstance?

9. Are you over-entertained? Does leisure dominate your time commitments?

10. Are you overly preoccupied with yourself? Do you serve others or serve yourself?

11. Do you posses a healthy amount of contest and conquest, strain and struggle or do you feel lost in softness and effeminacy? Explain.

Prayers

Observations

Revelations

Week 15: Dwell in the Shelter of the Most High

Find a beautiful place in nature to hold group. Get away from your normal meeting spot.

<u>Discussion Questions</u>:

Read Psalm 91, *""Whoever dwells in the shelter of the Most High will rest in the shadow of the Almighty. I will say of the Lord, "He is my refuge and my fortress, my God, in whom I trust." Surely he will save you from the fowler's snare and from the deadly pestilence. He will cover you with his feathers, and under his wings you will find refuge; his faithfulness will be your shield and rampart. You will not fear the terror of night, nor the arrow that flies by day, nor the pestilence that stalks in the darkness, nor the plague that destroys at midday. A thousand may fall at your side, ten thousand at your right hand, but it will not come near you. You will only observe with your eyes and see the punishment of the wicked. If you say, "The Lord is my refuge," and you make the Most High your dwelling, no harm will overtake you, no disaster will come near your tent. For he will command his angels concerning you to guard you in all your ways; they will lift you up in their hands, so that you will not strike your foot against a stone. You will tread on the lion and the cobra; you will trample the great lion and the serpent. "Because he loves me," says the Lord, "I will rescue him; I will protect him, for he acknowledges my name. He will call on me, and I will answer him; I will be with him in trouble, I will deliver him and honor him. With long life I will satisfy him and show him my salvation.""*

1. What does it mean to *"dwell in the shelter of the Most High?"*

2. What does it mean that the Lord will, *"cover you with His feathers?"*

3. The Psalmist uses several metaphors to describe how God will protect you. What does the need for protection say about the environment you are called to enter?

4. What in this verse gives you confidence to enter the proving ground?

5. Jesus clearly wasn't afraid to face the wilderness and the challenges it offered, but He also viewed the wilderness as a place to find respite. After feeding the 5,000, and likely exhausted, what did Jesus do? Read Matthew 14:23. *"After he had dismissed them, he went up on a mountainside by himself to pray. Later that night, he was there alone."* Why do you think he needed to be alone?

6. How did Jesus pray? Read Matthew 6:5-13… *""And when you pray, do not be like the hypocrites, for they love to pray standing in the synagogues and on the street corners to be seen by others. Truly I tell you, they have received their reward in full. But when you pray, go into your room, close the door and pray to your Father, who is unseen. Then your Father, who sees what is done in secret, will reward you. And when you pray, do not keep on babbling like pagans, for they think they will be heard because of their many words. Do not be like them, for your Father knows what you need before you ask him. "This, then, is how you should pray: " 'Our Father in heaven, hallowed be your name, your kingdom come, your will be done, on earth as it is in heaven. Give us today our daily bread. And forgive us our debts, as we also have forgiven our debtors. And lead us not into temptation, but deliver us from the evil one."* How can you use the Lord's Prayer to guide your prayer time?

Prayer Exercise: Spread out and find a quiet place. Pray specifically using the Lord's prayer as a guide. Record what you pray about in each section of the Lord's Prayer. When you are done, open your eyes and marvel at the beauty of your environment which was created by God. Then be still and listen to His voice.

Our Father in heaven, hallowed be your name:

Your kingdom come, your will be done, on earth as it is in heaven:

Give us today our daily bread:

And forgive us our debts, as we also have forgiven our debtors:

And lead us not into temptation, but deliver us from the evil one:

Challenge: Marvel at God's Creation

Spend at least 30 minutes a day outside and alone with zero distractions. It's gonna be difficult to cordon off the time...do it anyway. What do you notice about the world around you? What is right in front of you that you find beautiful or amazing? Pray using the Lord's Prayer as you guide.. Listen to God's voice. Write down what you prayed and what He reveals.

Day 1:
Our Father in heaven, hallowed be your name:

Your kingdom come, your will be done, on earth as it is in heaven:

Give us today our daily bread:

And forgive us our debts, as we also have forgiven our debtors:

And lead us not into temptation, but deliver us from the evil one:

Revelations:

Day 2:
Our Father in heaven, hallowed be your name:

Your kingdom come, your will be done, on earth as it is in heaven:

Give us today our daily bread:

And forgive us our debts, as we also have forgiven our debtors:

And lead us not into temptation, but deliver us from the evil one:

Revelations:

Day 3:
Our Father in heaven, hallowed be your name:

Your kingdom come, your will be done, on earth as it is in heaven:

Give us today our daily bread:

And forgive us our debts, as we also have forgiven our debtors:

And lead us not into temptation, but deliver us from the evil one:

Revelations:

Day 4:
Our Father in heaven, hallowed be your name:

Your kingdom come, your will be done, on earth as it is in heaven:

Give us today our daily bread:

And forgive us our debts, as we also have forgiven our debtors:

And lead us not into temptation, but deliver us from the evil one:

Revelations:

Day 5:
Our Father in heaven, hallowed be your name:

Your kingdom come, your will be done, on earth as it is in heaven:

Give us today our daily bread:

And forgive us our debts, as we also have forgiven our debtors:

And lead us not into temptation, but deliver us from the evil one:

Revelations:

Day 6:
Our Father in heaven, hallowed be your name:

Your kingdom come, your will be done, on earth as it is in heaven:

Give us today our daily bread:

And forgive us our debts, as we also have forgiven our debtors:

And lead us not into temptation, but deliver us from the evil one:

Revelations:

Day 7:
Our Father in heaven, hallowed be your name:

Your kingdom come, your will be done, on earth as it is in heaven:

Give us today our daily bread:

And forgive us our debts, as we also have forgiven our debtors:

And lead us not into temptation, but deliver us from the evil one:

Revelations:

Prayers

Observations

Revelations

Week 16: Walk with the Lord

Find a beautiful place in nature to hold group. Get away from your normal meeting spot.

Take a long walk alone. Reflect on revelations from the previous weeks challenges. Stop at a beautiful spot somewhere on the walk. Sit, be still, and hear the Lords voice. Review your purpose statement. Write down your latest version. Allow the Holy Spirit to amend or change any part of it. Record your updated purpose statement. Share with your accountability group.

Current Purpose Statement:

Revised Purpose Statement:

Challenge: Be Still and Know

Read chapter 8 (Craftsman) for discussion next week.

Spend at least 30 minutes a day outside and alone with zero distractions. It's gonna be difficult to cordon off the time…do it anyway.

Read Psalms 46:10. *"He says, "Be still, and know that I am God; I will be exalted among the nations, I will be exalted in the earth.""*

Be still and know…what do you notice about the world around you? What is right in front of you that is beautiful or amazing? This week focus on being still and silent so you can hear God's voice. Meditate on God's provision, God's beauty, and displaying gratitude. Record your prayers, observations, and revelations.

Prayers

Observations

Revelations

Week 17: You Are a Craftsman (Ch. 8)

Discussion questions:

1. What stood out about the chapter.

2. What are your favorite mediums of creativity? How do you like to be creative?

3. How do you feel when you get to exercise your creativity? Put another way...how does that activity make you feel when you get to do it?

4. Genesis describes our God who created the Heavens and the Earth and then created man and woman in His own image. The book describes the creative process in terms of making something that is a reflection of the designer (pg. 139). Can you relate to that? How does that make you feel about your connection to the creator?

5. The golden calf and Tower of Babel are both examples of men perverting creation to worship a thing in place of the living God. The book describes an idol as, *"anything we look to besides God to give us what only God can provide - identity, purpose, provision, protection, and worth"* (Pg. 140). What are your idols?

6. If our creative spirit is a gift from God, how does the Devil use it against us? Have you experienced this in your life?

7. Recount the story of Nebuchadnezzar.

"Then Daniel (also called Belteshazzar) was greatly perplexed for a time, and his thoughts terrified him. So the king said, "Belteshazzar, do not let the dream or its meaning alarm you." Belteshazzar answered, "My Lord, if only the dream applied to your enemies and its meaning to your adversaries! The tree you saw, which grew large and strong, with its top touching the sky, visible to the whole earth, with beautiful leaves and abundant fruit, providing food for all, giving shelter to the wild animals, and having nesting places in its branches for the birds— Your Majesty, you are that tree! You have become great and strong; your greatness has grown until it reaches the sky, and your dominion extends to distant parts of the earth. "Your Majesty saw a holy one, a messenger, coming down from heaven and saying, 'Cut down the tree and destroy it, but leave the stump, bound with iron and bronze, in the grass of the field, while its roots remain in the ground. Let him be drenched with the dew of heaven; let him live with the wild animals, until seven times pass by for him.' "This is the interpretation, Your Majesty, and this is the decree the Most High has issued against my Lord the king: You will be driven away from people and will live with the wild animals; you will eat grass like the ox and be drenched with the dew of heaven. Seven times will pass by for you until you acknowledge that the Most High is sovereign over all kingdoms on earth and gives them to anyone he wishes. The command to leave the stump of the tree with its roots means that your kingdom will be restored to you when you acknowledge that Heaven rules. Therefore, Your Majesty, be pleased to accept my advice: Renounce your sins by doing what is right, and your wickedness by being kind to the oppressed. It may be that then your prosperity will continue."" Daniel 4:19-27.

The King created a great Kingdom. Where did he go wrong?

SPIRITUAL GIFTS SURVEY

DIRECTIONS
This is not a test, so there are no wrong answers. The **Spiritual Gifts Survey** consists of 80 statements. Some items reflect concrete actions; other items are descriptive traits; and still others are statements of belief.

- Select the one response you feel best characterizes yourself and place that number in the blank provided. Record your answer in the blank beside each item.
- Do not spend too much time on any one item. Remember, it is not a test. Usually your immediate response is best.
- Please give an answer for each item. Do not skip any items.
- Do not ask others how they are answering or how they think you should answer.
- Work at your own pace.

Your response choices are:

5—Highly characteristic of me/definitely true for me
4—Most of the time this would describe me/be true for me
3—Frequently characteristic of me/true for me—about 50 percent of the time
2—Occasionally characteristic of me/true for me—about 25 percent of the time
1—Not at all characteristic of me/definitely untrue for me

_____ 1. I have the ability to organize ideas, resources, time, and people effectively.
_____ 2. I am willing to study and prepare for the task of teaching.
_____ 3. I am able to relate the truths of God to specific situations.
_____ 4. I have a God-given ability to help others grow in their faith.
_____ 5. I possess a special ability to communicate the truth of salvation.
_____ 6. I have the ability to make critical decisions when necessary.
_____ 7. I am sensitive to the hurts of people.
_____ 8. I experience joy in meeting needs through sharing possessions.
_____ 9. I enjoy studying.
_____ 10. I have delivered God's message of warning and judgment.
_____ 11. I am able to sense the true motivation of persons and movements.
_____ 12. I have a special ability to trust God in difficult situations.
_____ 13. I have a strong desire to contribute to the establishment of new churches.
_____ 14. I take action to meet physical and practical needs rather than merely talking about or planning to help.
_____ 15. I enjoy entertaining guests in my home.
_____ 16. I can adapt my guidance to fit the maturity of those working with me.
_____ 17. I can delegate and assign meaningful work.

Spiritual Gifts Survey
LifeWay Christian Resources

_____ 18. I have an ability and desire to teach.
_____ 19. I am usually able to analyze a situation correctly.
_____ 20. I have a natural tendency to encourage others.
_____ 21. I am willing to take the initiative in helping other Christians grow in their faith.
_____ 22. I have an acute awareness of the emotions of other people, such as loneliness, pain, fear, and anger.
_____ 23. I am a cheerful giver.
_____ 24. I spend time digging into facts.
_____ 25. I feel that I have a message from God to deliver to others.
_____ 26. I can recognize when a person is genuine/honest.
_____ 27. I am a person of vision (a clear mental portrait of a preferable future given by God). I am able to communicate vision in such a way that others commit to making the vision a reality.
_____ 28. I am willing to yield to God's will rather than question and waver.
_____ 29. I would like to be more active in getting the gospel to people in other lands.
_____ 30. It makes me happy to do things for people in need.
_____ 31. I am successful in getting a group to do its work joyfully.
_____ 32. I am able to make strangers feel at ease.
_____ 33. I have the ability to plan learning approaches.
_____ 34. I can identify those who need encouragement.
_____ 35. I have trained Christians to be more obedient disciples of Christ.
_____ 36. I am willing to do whatever it takes to see others come to Christ.
_____ 37. I am attracted to people who are hurting.
_____ 38. I am a generous giver.
_____ 39. I am able to discover new truths.
_____ 40. I have spiritual insights from Scripture concerning issues and people that compel me to speak out.
_____ 41. I can sense when a person is acting in accord with God's will.
_____ 42. I can trust in God even when things look dark.
_____ 43. I can determine where God wants a group to go and help it get there.
_____ 44. I have a strong desire to take the gospel to places where it has never been heard.
_____ 45. I enjoy reaching out to new people in my church and community.
_____ 46. I am sensitive to the needs of people.
_____ 47. I have been able to make effective and efficient plans for accomplishing the goals of a group.

Copyright © 2003 LifeWay Christian Resources

Spiritual Gifts Survey
LifeWay Christian Resources

____ 48. I often am consulted when fellow Christians are struggling to make difficult decisions.
____ 49. I think about how I can comfort and encourage others in my congregation.
____ 50. I am able to give spiritual direction to others.
____ 51. I am able to present the gospel to lost persons in such a way that they accept the Lord and His salvation.
____ 52. I possess an unusual capacity to understand the feelings of those in distress.
____ 53. I have a strong sense of stewardship based on the recognition that God owns all things.
____ 54. I have delivered to other persons messages that have come directly from God.
____ 55. I can sense when a person is acting under God's leadership.
____ 56. I try to be in God's will continually and be available for His use.
____ 57. I feel that I should take the gospel to people who have different beliefs from me.
____ 58. I have an acute awareness of the physical needs of others.
____ 59. I am skilled in setting forth positive and precise steps of action.
____ 60. I like to meet visitors at church and make them feel welcome.
____ 61. I explain Scripture in such a way that others understand it.
____ 62. I can usually see spiritual solutions to problems.
____ 63. I welcome opportunities to help people who need comfort, consolation, encouragement, and counseling.
____ 64. I feel at ease in sharing Christ with nonbelievers.
____ 65. I can influence others to perform to their highest God-given potential.
____ 66. I recognize the signs of stress and distress in others.
____ 67. I desire to give generously and unpretentiously to worthwhile projects and ministries.
____ 68. I can organize facts into meaningful relationships.
____ 69. God gives me messages to deliver to His people.
____ 70. I am able to sense whether people are being honest when they tell of their religious experiences.
____ 71. I enjoy presenting the gospel to persons of other cultures and backgrounds.
____ 72. I enjoy doing little things that help people.
____ 73. I can give a clear, uncomplicated presentation.
____ 74. I have been able to apply biblical truth to the specific needs of my church.
____ 75. God has used me to encourage others to live Christlike lives.
____ 76. I have sensed the need to help other people become more effective in their ministries.

Copyright © 2003 LifeWay Christian Resources

Spiritual Gifts Survey
LifeWay Christian Resources

_____ 77. I like to talk about Jesus to those who do not know Him.

_____ 78. I have the ability to make strangers feel comfortable in my home.

_____ 79. I have a wide range of study resources and know how to secure information.

_____ 80. I feel assured that a situation will change for the glory of God even when the situation seem impossible.

Scoring Your Survey

Follow these directions to figure your score for each spiritual gift.

1. Place in each box your numerical response (1-5) to the item number which is indicated below the box.
2. For each gift, add the numbers in the boxes and put the total in the TOTAL box.

LEADERSHIP	___	+	___	+	___	+	___	+	___	=	___
	Item 6		Item 16		Item 27		Item 43		Item 65		TOTAL
ADMINISTRATION	___	+	___	+	___	+	___	+	___	=	___
	Item 1		Item 17		Item 31		Item 47		Item 59		TOTAL
TEACHING	___	+	___	+	___	+	___	+	___	=	___
	Item 2		Item 18		Item 33		Item 61		Item 73		TOTAL
KNOWLEDGE	___	+	___	+	___	+	___	+	___	=	___
	Item 9		Item 24		Item 39		Item 68		Item 79		TOTAL
WISDOM	___	+	___	+	___	+	___	+	___	=	___
	Item 3		Item 19		Item 48		Item 62		Item 74		TOTAL
PROPHECY	___	+	___	+	___	+	___	+	___	=	___
	Item 10		Item 25		Item 40		Item 54		Item 69		TOTAL
DISCERNMENT	___	+	___	+	___	+	___	+	___	=	___
	Item 11		Item 26		Item 41		Item 55		Item 70		TOTAL
EXHORTATION	___	+	___	+	___	+	___	+	___	=	___
	Item 20		Item 34		Item 49		Item 63		Item 75		TOTAL
SHEPHERDING	___	+	___	+	___	+	___	+	___	=	___
	Item 4		Item 21		Item 35		Item 50		Item 76		TOTAL
FAITH	___	+	___	+	___	+	___	+	___	=	___
	Item 12		Item 28		Item 42		Item 56		Item 80		TOTAL
EVANGELISM	___	+	___	+	___	+	___	+	___	=	___
	Item 5		Item 36		Item 51		Item 64		Item 77		TOTAL
APOSTLESHIP	___	+	___	+	___	+	___	+	___	=	___
	Item 13		Item 29		Item 44		Item 57		Item 71		TOTAL
SERVICE/HELPS	___	+	___	+	___	+	___	+	___	=	___
	Item 14		Item 30		Item 46		Item 58		Item 72		TOTAL
MERCY	___	+	___	+	___	+	___	+	___	=	___
	Item 7		Item 22		Item 37		Item 52		Item 66		TOTAL
GIVING	___	+	___	+	___	+	___	+	___	=	___
	Item 8		Item 23		Item 38		Item 53		Item 67		TOTAL
HOSPITALITY	___	+	___	+	___	+	___	+	___	=	___
	Item 15		Item 32		Item 45		Item 60		Item 78		TOTAL

Copyright © 2003 LifeWay Christian Resources

Spiritual Gifts Survey
LifeWay Christian Resources

GRAPHING YOUR PROFILE

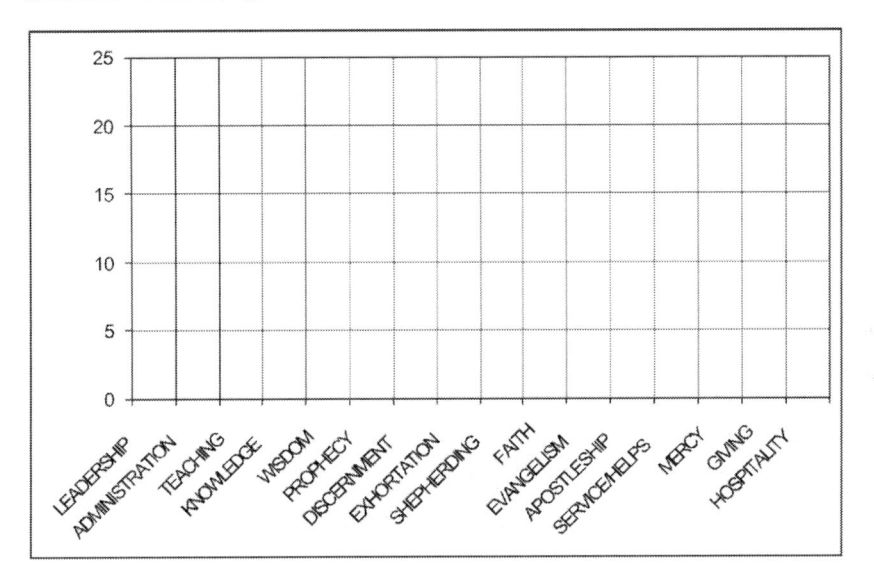

[Bar graph with y-axis scale 0, 5, 10, 15, 20, 25 and x-axis categories: LEADERSHIP, ADMINISTRATION, TEACHING, KNOWLEDGE, WISDOM, PROPHECY, DISCERNMENT, EXHORTATION, SHEPHERDING, FAITH, EVANGELISM, APOSTLESHIP, SERVICE/HELPS, MERCY, GIVING, HOSPITALITY]

1. For each gift place a mark across the bar at the point that corresponds to your TOTAL for that gift.
2. For each gift shade the bar below the mark that you have drawn.
3. The resultant graph gives a picture of your gifts. Gifts for which the bars are tall are the ones in which you appear to be strongest. Gifts for which the bars are very short are the ones in which you appear not to be strong.

Now that you have completed the survey, thoughtfully answer the following questions.

The gifts I have begun to discover in my life are:
1. _____
2. _____
3. _____

- After prayer and worship, I am beginning to sense that God wants me to use my spiritual gifts to serve Christ's body by _____.
- I am not sure yet how God wants me to use my gifts to serve others. But I am committed to prayer and worship, seeking wisdom and opportunities to use the gifts I have received from God.

Ask God to help you know how He has gifted you for service and how you can begin to use this gift in ministry to others.

Copyright © 2003 LifeWay Christian Resources

Spiritual Gifts List
LifeWay Christian Resources

Discover Your Spiritual Gifts!
Gene Wilkes

Ken Hemphill defines a spiritual gift as "an individual manifestation of grace from the Father that enables you to serve Him and thus play a vital role in His plan for the redemption of the world."[i] Peter Wagner defines a spiritual gift as "a special attribute given by the Holy Spirit to every member of the Body of Christ according to God's grace for use within the context of the Body."[ii] I like to use this definition:

A spiritual gift is an expression of the Holy Spirit in the life of believers which empowers them to serve the body of Christ, the church.

Romans 12:6-8; 1 Corinthians 12:8-10, 28-30; Ephesians 4:11; and 1 Peter 4:9-11 contain representative lists of gifts and roles God has given to the church. A definition of these gifts follows.[iii]

Leadership - Leadership aids the body by leading and directing members to accomplish the goals and purposes of the church. Leadership motivates people to work together in unity toward common goals (Rom. 12:8).

Administration - Persons with the gift of administration lead the body by steering others to remain on task. Administration enables the body to organize according to God-given purposes and long-term goals (1 Cor. 12:28).

Teaching - Teaching is instructing members in the truths and doctrines of God's Word for the purposes of building up, unifying, and maturing the body (1 Cor. 12:28; Rom. 12:7; Eph. 4:11).

Knowledge - The gift of knowledge manifests itself in teaching and training in discipleship. It is the God-given ability to learn, know, and explain the precious truths of God's Word. A word of knowledge is a Spirit-revealed truth (1 Cor. 12:28).

Wisdom - Wisdom is the gift that discerns the work of the Holy Spirit in the body and applies His teachings and actions to the needs of the body (1 Cor. 12:28).

Prophecy - The gift of prophecy is proclaiming the Word of God boldly. This builds up the body and leads to conviction of sin. Prophecy manifests itself in preaching and teaching (1 Cor. 12:10; Rom. 12:6).

Discernment - Discernment aids the body by recognizing the true intentions of those within or related to the body. Discernment tests the message and actions of others for the protection and well-being of the body (1 Cor. 12:10).

Exhortation - Possessors of this gift encourage members to be involved in and enthusiastic about the work of the Lord. Members with this gift are good counselors and motivate others to service. Exhortation exhibits itself in preaching, teaching, and ministry (Rom. 12:8).

Copyright © 2003 LifeWay Christian Resources

Shepherding - The gift of shepherding is manifested in persons who look out for the spiritual welfare of others. Although pastors, like shepherds, do care for members of the church, this gift is not limited to a pastor or staff member (Eph. 4:11).

Faith - Faith trusts God to work beyond the human capabilities of the people. Believers with this gift encourage others to trust in God in the face of apparently insurmountable odds (1 Cor. 12:9).

Evangelism - God gifts his church with evangelists to lead others to Christ effectively and enthusiastically. This gift builds up the body by adding new members to its fellowship (Eph. 4:11).

Apostleship - The church sends apostles from the body to plant churches or be missionaries. Apostles motivate the body to look beyond its walls in order to carry out the Great Commission (1 Cor. 12:28; Eph. 4:11).

Service/Helps - Those with the gift of service/helps recognize practical needs in the body and joyfully give assistance to meeting those needs. Christians with this gift do not mind working behind the scenes (1 Cor. 12:28; Rom. 12:7).

Mercy - Cheerful acts of compassion characterize those with the gift of mercy. Persons with this gift aid the body by empathizing with hurting members. They keep the body healthy and unified by keeping others aware of the needs within the church (Rom. 12:8).

Giving - Members with the gift of giving give freely and joyfully to the work and mission of the body. Cheerfulness and liberality are characteristics of individuals with this gift (Rom. 12:8).

Hospitality - Those with this gift have the ability to make visitors, guests, and strangers feel at ease. They often use their home to entertain guests. Persons with this gift integrate new members into the body (1 Pet. 4:9).

God has gifted you with an expression of His Holy Spirit to support His vision and mission of the church. It is a worldwide vision to reach all people with the gospel of Christ. As a servant leader, God desires that you know how He has gifted you. This will lead you to where He would have you serve as part of His vision and mission for the church.

Download the Spiritual Gifts Survey from LifeWay.com.

Gene Wilkes is pastor of Legacy Church, Plano, Texas. This article was adapted from Jesus on Leadership: Developing Servant Leaders, by Gene Wilkes (LifeWay Christian Resources 1998).

---

[i] Ken Hemphill, *Serving God: Discovering and Using Your Spiritual Gifts Workbook* (Dallas: The Sampson Company, 1995), 22.

[ii] *Your Spiritual Gifts Can Help Your Church Grow* by C. Peter Wagner, Copyright © 1979, Regal Books, Ventura, CA 93003. Used by permission, 42.

[iii] These definitions exclude the "sign gifts" because of some confusion that accompanies these gifts and because they are difficult to fit into ministries within a typical church's ministry base.

Copyright © 2003 LifeWay Christian Resources

8. How was Jesus different? Share your thoughts from the chapter (pg. 146-148).

9. What do you think of the concept of using our wounds/scars to inspire our creativity?

10. So what's the point? Why are we called to create? What's holding you back?

Challenge: Spiritual Gifts Assessment

This week spend some time with the God to identify the ways you are called to be creative. Also ask Him to identify the idols in your life and the things that prevent you from using your creativity to advance God's Kingdom. Take the attached spiritual gifts assessment and be prepared to discuss next week.

1. What areas am I called to be creative?

2. What idols has the Holy Spirit revealed in my life

Prayers

__Observations__

Revelations

Week 18: Spiritual Gifts Discussion

Discussion Questions:

1. Chris Hodges defines a spiritual gift as, "A special supernatural ability that God gives to each of His children, so that together they can advance His purposes in this world." What is your definition?

2. How does scripture define spiritual gifts?

"There are different kinds of gifts, but the same Spirit distributes them. There are different kinds of service, but the same Lord. There are different kinds of working, but in all of them and in everyone it is the same God at work. Now to each one the manifestation of the Spirit is given for the common good. To one there is given through the Spirit a message of wisdom, to another a message of knowledge by means of the same Spirit, to another faith by the same Spirit, to another gifts of healing by that one Spirit, to another miraculous powers, to another prophecy, to another distinguishing between spirits, to another speaking in different kinds of tongues, and to still another the interpretation of tongues. All these are the work of one and the same Spirit, and he distributes them to each one, just as he determines." 1 Corinthians 12:4-11.

According to the scripture, do we all have spiritual gifts?

3. Read 1 Corinthians 12:21-26. *"The eye cannot say to the hand, "I don't need you!" And the head cannot say to the feet, "I don't need you!" On the contrary, those parts of the body that seem to be weaker are indispensable, and the parts that we think are less honorable we treat with special honor. And the parts that are unpresentable are treated with special modesty, while our presentable parts need no special treatment. But God has put the body together, giving greater honor to the parts that lacked it, so that there should be no division in the body, but that its parts should have equal concern for each other. If one part suffers, every part suffers with it; if one part is honored, every part rejoices with it."* What does scripture say about the value of each spiritual gift? How does that relate to the value of your purpose to Christ's church?

4. Read Romans 1:11-12. *"I long to see you so that I may impart to you some spiritual gift to make you strong— that is, that you and I may be mutually encouraged by each other's faith."*

Read Romans 12:3-8. *"For by the grace given me I say to every one of you: Do not think of yourself more highly than you ought, but rather think of yourself with sober judgment, in accordance with the faith God has distributed to each of you. For just as each of us has one body with many members, and these members do not all have the same function, so in Christ we, though many, form one body, and each member belongs to all the others. We have different gifts, according to the grace given to each of us. If your gift is prophesying, then prophesy in accordance with your faith; if it is serving, then serve; if it is teaching, then teach; if it is to encourage, then give encouragement; if it is giving, then give generously; if it is to lead, do it diligently; if it is to show mercy, do it cheerfully."*

How did God intend for us to use our spiritual gifts to effect His church?

5. Read 1 Peter 4:10-11. *"Each of you should use whatever gift you have received to serve others, as faithful stewards of God's grace in its various forms. If anyone speaks, they should do so as one who speaks the very words of God. If anyone serves, they should do so with the strength God provides, so that in all things God may be praised through Jesus Christ. To him be the glory and the power for ever and ever. Amen."* What is God's command for your spiritual gifts?

6. Read Matthew 25:25-26, 28-30. *"So I was afraid and went out and hid your gold in the ground. See, here is what belongs to you.' "His master replied, 'You wicked, lazy servant! So you knew that I harvest where I have not sown and gather where I have not scattered seed? " 'So take the bag of gold from him and give it to the one who has ten bags. For whoever has will be given more, and they will have an abundance. Whoever does not have, even what they have will be taken from them. And throw that worthless servant outside, into the darkness, where there will be weeping and gnashing of teeth.'"* What happens to those who ignore their spiritual gifts? What happens to those who use them wisely?

7. In Billy Graham's book "The Holy Spirit," he states, "*He (the Holy Spirit) chooses who gets which gifts, and He dispenses them at His good pleasure. While we are held accountable for the use of any gifts He gives us, we have no responsibility for gifts we have not been given.*" What is Reverend Graham saying about the spirit of comparison?

8. Share your top 3 and bottom three spiritual gifts with the group.

Top Spiritual Gift:_____

Second Spiritual Gift:_____

Third Spiritual Gift: _____

Lowest Scored Spiritual Gift:_____

Second Lowest Spiritual Gift:_____

Third Lowest Spiritual Gift: _____

Are there any surprises in your scores? Explain:

9. Take note of who in the group is strong in the spiritual gifts you are weak in…for future networking opportunities.

Challenge: Dream Big

Spend some time with God and answer the following questions (These are open ended and general on purpose).

1. If you could build your perfect church from scratch, what would it look like?

2. What are your spiritual gifts?

First:_____

Second:_____

Third: _____

What ministry is God calling you into right now?

3. What is your "Big Dream" in life?

4. If you could share one skill you have with the world, what would it be? Why?

Prayers

Observations

Revelations

Week 19: Say It Out Loud, Share Your Gifts

Discussion Questions:

1. Share the answers to last weeks challenge questions with the group.
- If you could build your perfect church from scratch, what would it look like?
- What ministry is God calling you into right now?
- What is your "Big Dream" in life?
- If you could share one skill you have with the world, what would it be?

2. What aspects of other members "Perfect Church" do you want to incorporate into yours?

3. Is anyone in the group being called into a similar ministry? Who and what?

4. Does anyone in the group have a similar "Big Dream"? Are there any networking opportunities you can leverage? Is there anyone you can help realize their dream? Explain:

5. What skills shared by the group do you want to learn? Describe:

Challenge: Build Week

Read Chapter 9 (Leader) for discussion next week.

Exercise your creative juices. As a group, design a build project. Make plans to setup a workshop so everyone can work with their hands to build something tangible they can take home. Viking chairs have been a popular build because they are easy to do, customizable, and you can bring them to Junto events. This exercise is a great way for skilled men to teach those who haven't ever worked with their hands. Make an attempt to include all the skills shared by the group. Pick a time as a group and make it happen.

Take your answers from the last three weeks to the God. Compare them to your purpose statement. Make changes to your purpose statement if applicable. Share your new purpose statement with your accountability partners.

Current Purpose Statement:

Revised Purpose Statement:

Prayers

Observations

Revelations

Week 20: You Are a Leader (Ch. 9)

Discussion Questions:

1. Who is someone you respect as a leader? Why?

2. Recall the story of David and the concept of the ever increasing dominos. How does it make you feel to know our decisions can have great effect on others?

3. As a leader is it intimidating or exciting to know our decisions may have huge impacts on those around us? Explain.

4. How does the clash between Heavenly forgiveness and earthly consequences effect your decision making process?

5. How does the Devil use shame and fear to prevent you from becoming the leader you are called to be?

6. Read John 10:14-18. *""I am the good shepherd; I know my sheep and my sheep know me—just as the Father knows me and I know the Father—and I lay down my life for the sheep. I have other sheep that are not of this sheep pen. I must bring them also. They too will listen to my voice, and there shall be one flock and one shepherd. The reason my Father loves me is that I lay down my life—only to take it up again. No one takes it from me, but I lay it down of my own accord. I have authority to lay it down and authority to take it up again. This command I received from my Father.""*

Jesus was a man who was neither impressed by people's favor, nor intimidated by their jealousy. Which leadership qualities, that Jesus demonstrated on page 168, do you want to emulate? What do you need to change about your leadership style after considering Jesus' example

7. As a flawed man, how can you lead with God's very heart?

8. What specific steps can you take to lead from God's very heart in your own family?

Challenge: Find Your Swim Lane

As men we should seek eloquent ways to lead from any position (peer, subordinate, or supervisor). Different tools and styles are needed for each relationship. Recall the swim lane metaphor whereby Navy SEALS use their strengths/roles to lead effectively. *"First, they have high levels of clarity and commitment to the team and to their mission, purpose, and vision. Second, each team member knows their strengths and weaknesses and leads from where they stand on the team"* (Seek. Adapt. Endure, pg.70).

We are all called and capable of leading. Leadership is ultimately about serving others through sacrificial love. Yes, we are still imperfect humans, but when we are leaning into God and leaning toward others with love and faithfulness, there is grace to learn from our mistakes and see God redeem them. So let's lean in.

This week reflect inward on your leadership strengths…find your swim lane…and work to improve. Answer the following questions.

1. What are the qualities of an effective leader?

2. What are 2 qualities about you that make you an effective leader?

3. What are 2 things you can improve to become a more effective leader?

4. As a servant leader, what are the things you need to do for the people most important to you (In your role as a Husband/Dad/Son/Friend/etc)?

Prayers

Observations

Revelations

Week 21: Leaders Create Safe Environments

Watched the Simon Sinek YouTube video entitled, "Why good leaders make you feel safe."

https://youtu.be/lmyZMtPVodo?si=490MbyyJUJ_eik0M

Discussion Questions:

1. How do the principles in this video apply to your family?

2. How do the principles in this video apply to your friend groups?

3. How do the principles in this video apply to your community?

4. How do the principles in this video apply to your church?

5. What are some ways we can motivate people behind a common purpose?

6. Tools of an effective leader workshop. For the rest of session, as a group, answer the question, "What are the qualities of a good leader?" Have one person write down everyone's input on a white board or digital screen for everyone to see. Record the list below to meditate over later. Highlight qualities you never considered before.

Challenge: Seek Honest Feedback

Poll your friends and family. Give 3-4 people a copy of the following questions and ask them to give you honest/constructive feedback. Reflect on their answers and identify areas of strength and weakness. Write down their answers and compare to how you answered these questions last week.

1. What are the qualities of an effective leader?
2. What are 2 qualities about me that make me an effective leader?
3. What are 2 things I can improve to become a more effective leader?
4. As a servant leader, what are the things I need to do for you in my role as your Husband/Dad/Son/Friend/etc?

After collecting responses, input the highlights in the attached matrix for comparison.

Leadership Feedback Poll

	What are the qualities of an effective leader?	What are 2 qualities about me that make me an effective leader?	What are 2 things I can improve to become a more effective leader?	As a servant leader, what are the things I need to do for you in my role as your _____?
My Answers				
Name:				
Name:				
Name:				

Prayers

Observations

Revelations

Week 22: Leadership Panel

The purpose of the leadership panel is to gather different perspectives that incorporate the concept of 360 degree leadership. The goal is to hear as many different perspectives on leadership to add tools to our individual toolkit and understand how our leadership style needs to change to meet the individual situation. Remember, your leadership style is not always the best and you can learn from others to be more effective…so keep an open mind.

Panel Members (4 person panel is desirable):
- An elder of the church: Someone older and mature in their faith.
- Married Couple: Purpose is to speak to the leadership challenges that exist in the marriage relationship and how to lead as one flesh within your family and community. Also provides a female perspective to leadership.
- Teen: Provide perspective from the younger generation.

Panel Questions:

1. For everyone: Excluding Jesus, who is one person you admire for their leadership abilities and why?

2. For everyone: In John 13:34-35, Jesus said, *"A new command I give you: Love one another. As I have loved you, so you must love one another. By this everyone will know that you are my disciples, if you love one another."* How do the elemental properties of love, as Christ defined, inform your leadership tactics as a leader in your environment (home, workplace, etc)?

3. For everyone: Jeremiah 17:10 says, *"I the Lord search the heart and examine the mind, to reward each person according to their conduct, according to what their deeds deserve."* Our spiritual endeavor is to reflect the heart of Jesus in our heart, mind and deeds. And yet often the content of our heart and our mind is not always coming from that place of love. With that in mind, what have been the most effective strategies for you to manage your emotions during conflict to ensure the gospel continues to be reflected as you lead others?

4. For everyone: Bonhoeffer said that the greatest act of love between two men is that of reprimand so as it relates to holding someone accountable or reprimanding them for poor performance or poor behavior? How do you strike the balance between grace and truth?

5. For the Elder: Jesus washed feet. He was willing to lower himself to a subordinate position to serve others from love. In what ways have you found it possible to be a leader from a position of inexperience ie. a subordinate position?

6. <u>For the Married Man</u>: The Pareto principle or the 80-20 rule, posits that 80% of a leader's time is spent on 20% of the problem causers. How do you ensure your time as a leader isn't disproportionately consumed managing problems or problematic people?

7. <u>For the Married Woman</u>: Within Jesus' disciples and even his closest three He dealt with wildly contrasting temperaments. An essential element of Godly leadership is meeting a person where they're at spiritually and psychologically and vectoring your leadership from there. What tactics and strategies as a leader have you found effective at handling the various temperaments within your home and your workplace?

8. <u>For the Teen</u>: It seems that there are many people in our current culture that are struggling to find their identity and purpose in life. We hear stories of high school kids and college kids getting into trouble with sex, alcohol, drugs, etc. How do you keep your heart centered on Jesus and keep from falling into these cultural struggles?

9. <u>For Everyone</u>: How do you balance your need for personal time and rejuvenation with the demands of school, work, sports and family? What strategies and tactics have you found effective in regards to rest, recovery and healing?

10. <u>For the Elder and the Married Man</u>: How do you intentionally seek to model the heart of Jesus within the confines of your marriage and how you treat your wife? As a followup: how does your wife KNOW that you love her through your actions?

11. <u>For the Married Woman</u>: What is your routine for including Jesus in your work and family decisions?

12. <u>For the Teen</u>: Where do you find inspiration for keeping your heart and mind focused on Jesus, working hard, and staying committed to the goals you've set in life.

13. <u>For Everyone</u>: Do you have any wounds (mental, spiritual, or physical) from your past that created strife and struggle with people in your family or workplace? If so, how did you overcome them?

14. <u>For Everyone</u>: What does it mean to you to be a servant leader?

15. <u>For Everyone</u>: What are the qualities/attributes you admire about effective leaders in your life? What is it about them that makes them so easy to follow?

16. <u>For Everyone</u>: What turns you off about ineffective leaders?

17. <u>For Everyone</u>: Do you find yourself leading your family (wife, kids, siblings, etc) with the same attention, energy, and motivation as you lead your teams outside the home? Do you work just as hard at pulling the full potential out of your family as you do your team?

The panel can be done in about an hour. If you plan more time for your discussion, consider doing breakouts. Break the guys into three groups. Each group will get 20 minutes with each panel member to ask specific questions. The following are ice breakers to get the discussion going. If you don't do breakouts you can use these questions for the overall panel.

1. For the Elder: what has been your biggest leadership challenge? What scriptures did you lean on to overcome that challenge?

2. For the Married Couple: Ephesians 5:21-33 says, *"Submit to one another out of reverence for Christ. Wives, submit yourselves to your own husbands as you do to the Lord. For the husband is the head of the wife as Christ is the head of the church, his body, of which he is the Savior. Now as the church submits to Christ, so also wives should submit to their husbands in everything. Husbands, love your wives, just as Christ loved the church and gave himself up for her to make her holy, cleansing her by the washing with water through the word, and to present her to himself as a radiant church, without stain or wrinkle or any other blemish, but holy and blameless. In this same way, husbands ought to love their wives as their own bodies. He who loves his wife loves himself. After all, no one ever hated their own body, but they feed and care for their body, just as Christ does the church—for we are members of his body. "For this reason a man will leave his father and mother and be united to his wife, and the two will become one flesh." This is a profound mystery—but I am talking about Christ and the church. However, each one of you also must love his wife as he loves himself, and the wife must respect her husband."* What does this verse mean to you and how have you applied it practically in your marriage?

3. For the Teen: What is one piece of advice you would give adult men about leading teenagers? What is one piece of advice you'd give teenagers about interacting with adults?

Challenge: Called Not Qualified

Read Chapter 10 (Be a Man of Action) for discussion next week.

What is the biggest reason men avoid their role as a leader? Confidence and fear of failure. The biggest excuse, "I don't know enough to lead a small group." True...none of us do. None of us know as much as Jesus and none of us ever will. There is still a place in His church for you to lead.

This week lead a devotional of your choice. Find someone in your life that will give you a chance to practice, pick a topic, and lead one discussion. Tips for success:
- Pick a topic or verse that can be researched quickly and discussed over one session.
- Pick a topic you are familiar with.
- Keep the group small. It can even be one on one. Make sure the group understands you are trying to practice leading discussion.
- Ask for honest feedback, delivered in a way that won't crush your spirit.
- Try leading a quick daily devotional with your family around the dinner table.
- Try to get the people in the group to talk more than you. Your goal is to lead discussion, not preach a sermon.
- Be brave and challenge yourself. It's OK to be uncomfortable...that's how you learn and grow.
- Just let God move. When in doubt, allow the Lord to take over.

Record a brief description of what you did, observations about your performance, what you learned from the exercise, and any revelations from God. Remember...God doesn't call the qualified, He qualifies the called.

1. Devotional Description:

2. Observations about my performance:

3. Lessons learned from this exercise:

4. Revelations from my leadership attempt:

Prayers

Observations

Revelations

Week 23: Be a Man of Action (Ch. 10)

Discussion questions:

1. Read Ernest Shackleton's recruitment add for the expedition to the arctic.

> MEN WANTED for hazardous journey, small wages, bitter cold, long months of complete darkness, constant danger, safe return doubtful, honor and recognition in case of success.
> Ernest Shackleton 4 Burlington st.

Would this add peak your interest? What about it appeals to you as a man?

2. Regarding Shackleton's crew…On page 177, Mike Sanders says, "*I can only imagine the incredible fear and doubt that swirled inside those men's hearts. Nevertheless, ready or not, they went. They went because they were men of action.*" Have you ever felt unprepared to step into God's calling? Can we ever feel 100% ready?

3. Over the course of the year, God has revealed something to you about your calling. Do you feel ready to answer the call? What practical steps can you take to become a man of action?

4. On page 178, Mike Sanders says, "*Please understand, God did not put His beloved image-bearers, His sons and daughters, on earth to survive. He put us here to thrive.*" What practical steps can we take as image-bearers of Christ to transition from nearly surviving life to abundantly thriving?

5. Go Forth, you are a Disciple. List 2 of your strengths and 2 of your weaknesses in your calling as a Disciple.

Disciple Strength:

Disciple Strength:

Disciple Weakness:

Disciple Weakness:

6. Live usefully, you are a Servant. List 2 of your strengths and 2 of your weaknesses in your calling as a Servant.

Servant Strength:

Servant Strength:

Servant Weakness:

Servant Weakness:

7. Live with purpose, you are a Warrior. List 2 of your strengths and 2 of your weaknesses in your calling as a Warrior.

Warrior Strength:

Warrior Strength:

Warrior Weakness:

Warrior Weakness:

8. Challenge intentionally, you are a Scholar. List 2 strengths and 2 weaknesses in your calling as a Scholar.

Scholar Strength:

Scholar Strength:

Scholar Weakness:

Scholar Weakness:

9. Discover new lands, you are an Explorer. List 2 strengths and 2 weaknesses in your calling as an Explorer.

Explorer Strength:

Explorer Strength:

Explorer Weakness:

Explorer Weakness:

10. Create joyfully, you are a Craftsman. List 2 strengths and 2 weaknesses in your calling as a Craftsman.

Craftsman Strength:

Craftsman Strength:

Craftsman Weakness:

Craftsman Weakness:

11. Be an inspiration, you are a Leader. List 2 strengths and 2 weaknesses in your calling as a Leader.

Leader Strength:

Leader Strength:

Leader Weakness:

Leader Weakness:

Challenge: Choose Your Hard

Archetype Applications:

Men of Action are men who constantly look at who they want to become (*seek*), identify and put in the focused, strategic work to close the gap (*adapt*), and continue to work this process their whole lives (*endure*). It's time to develop your holistic training plan to step into your calling in Christ.

We started this year developing your purpose statement. We explored God's plan for us as a Disciple, Servant, Scholar, Warrior, Craftsman, Explorer & Leader. After assessing your strengths and weaknesses, develop a holistic plan to become the man God wants you to be. Remember to consider your need to exercise all three aspects of your Tripartite Nature (Soul, Body, Spirit).

Over the course of the next two weeks, plan and execute a mini-application for each of the seven archetypes. Share with the group, combine ideas with other men, encourage your families to participate, and invite God to move through each application. Listen to the Holy Spirit and make final adjustments to your purpose statement. Complete this assignment before the "Call to Arms" event.

1. Disciple
Event Description:

Execution Date: _____

Required Materials:

Participants:

2. <u>Servant</u>
Event Description:

Execution Date: _____

Required Materials:

Participants:

3. <u>Warrior</u>
Event Description:

Execution Date: _____

Required Materials:

Participants:

4. <u>Scholar</u>
Event Description:

Execution Date: _____

Required Materials:

Participants:

5. <u>Explorer</u>
Event Description:

Execution Date: _____

Required Materials:

Participants:

6. <u>Craftsman</u>
Event Description:

Execution Date: _____

Required Materials:

Participants:

7. <u>Leader</u>
Event Description:

Execution Date: _____

Required Materials:

Participants:

Prayers

Observations

Revelations

Week 24: This is a Call to Arms!!!

"Jesus came and told his disciples, "I have been given all authority in heaven and on earth. Therefore, go and make disciples of all the nations, baptizing them in the name of the Father and the Son and the Holy Spirit. Teach these new disciples to obey all the commands I have given you. And be sure of this: I am with you always, even to the end of the age."" Matthew 28:18-20

"So now I am giving you a new commandment: Love each other. Just as I have loved you, you should love each other. Your love for one another will prove to the world that you are my disciples."" John 13:34-35

It's time to live out your purpose…not for love but from love. We are called to usher the Kingdom of Heaven to earth. We are called to make disciples for kingdom purpose. We are called to be the men God intended us to be. We are called to be love. Don't forget to live your life in purpose. Be a man of action.

<u>Final Draft Purpose Statement</u>

_____
_____
_____
_____
_____
_____
_____
_____
_____
_____
_____
_____
_____
_____
_____

Recommended Books/Online Resources

Next best steps

Sign up for Junto Tribe Marriage curriculum. Be the husband and father God intended you to be. Learn how to find purpose in your marriage the way God intended it...as one flesh.

Websites

For additional information visit our website at www.juntotribe.com. See our calendar of events that include life group applications, marriage groups, weekend "Infil" experiences, marriage retreats and seminars, group/personal training opportunities, blogs, podcasts, and opt in e-mail content.

Subscribe, Like, Follow, and Share our regular social media content on Instagram and Facebook.

Recommended Books

"Beautiful Outlaw" by John Eldredge

"The Ruthless Elimination of Hurry" by John Mark Comer

Courses

See the website for additional training courses coming soon.

Made in the USA
Columbia, SC
10 August 2024

7c34a887-e53f-4864-94f1-996c676dad80R01